The Diwan

of the Shaykh and Gnostic of Allah
Sayyidi Muhammad ibn al-Habib
al-Amghari al-Idrisi al-Hasani

The Diwan

of the Shaykh and Gnostic of Allah
Sayyidi Muhammad ibn al-Habib
al-Amghari al-Idrisi al-Hasani

*The Desire of Journeying Murids
and the Gift to Wayfaring Gnostics*

THE WIRD AND THE QASIDAS

DIWAN PRESS
Classical and Contemporary Books on Islam and Sufism

The Diwan of Shaykh Muhammad ibn al-Habib – The Wird and the Qasidas

Published by:	Iqra Agencies Ltd.
	P.O.Box 34027
	Erasmia
	0023
	South Africa
Website:	www.iqra.co.za
E-mail:	musa@iqra.co.za

Author: Shaykh Muhammad ibn al-Habib
Editors: Shaykh Murtada al-Boumas-houli and Abdassamad Clarke

A catalogue record of this book is available from the British Library.

ISBN-13:   978-1-908892-24-9 (Case laminate)

Contents

وَهَذَا وِرْدُنَا الشَّرِيفُ لِمَنْ أَرَادَهُ وَطَلَبَهُ فَهُوَ كَفِيلٌ بِكُلِّ خَيْرٍ
دَافِعٌ لِكُلِّ شَرٍّ وَبِالْمُوَاظَبَةِ عَلَيْهِ بِإِذْنٍ مِنَ الشَّيْخِ أَوِ الْمُقَدَّمِ
الْمَأْذُونِ مِنَ الشَّيْخِ يَجْمَعُ اللهُ لِلْعَبْدِ بَيْنَ الشَّرِيعَةِ وَالْحَقِيقَةِ
ونصه:

This is our noble Wird for whoever wishes it and seeks it.
Its recital guarantees every good and repels every evil.

If the slave perseveres in it with idhn from the Shaykh,
or from a muqaddam who has idhn from the Shaykh,
Allah will unite the Shari‘a and Haqiqa for him.

The Wird

مِفْتَاحُ الْوِرْدِ

The Key to the Wird

اَللّٰهُمَّ صَلِّ عَلَى سَيِّدِنَا مُحَمَّدٍ عَبْدِكَ وَرَسُولِكَ النَّبِيِّ الْأُمِّيِّ وَعَلَى ءَالِهِ وَصَحْبِهِ وَسَلِّمْ تَسْلِيمًا. عَدَدَ خَلْقِكَ وَرِضَا نَفْسِكَ وَزِنَةَ عَرْشِكَ وَمِدَادَ كَلِمَاتِكَ.

O Allah pour blessings upon our master Muhammad, Your slave and Messenger, the unlettered Prophet, and upon his Family and Companions and grant them perfect peace, as great as the number of Your creations and Your pleasure and the weight of Your throne and the ink of Your words.

أَعُوذُ بِاللّٰهِ السَّمِيعِ الْعَلِيمِ مِنَ الشَّيْطَانِ الرَّجِيمِ.

I take refuge with Allah, the All-Hearing, the All-Knowing from the accursed shaytan.

بِسْمِ اللّٰهِ الرَّحْمٰنِ الرَّحِيمِ

In the name of Allah, the All-Merciful, the Most Merciful

وَلَا حَوْلَ وَلَا قُوَّةَ إِلَّا بِاللّٰهِ الْعَلِيِّ الْعَظِيمِ.

There is no power and no strength but by Allah, the High, the Vast.

أَسْتَغْفِرُ اللهَ. (ثلاثا)

I seek forgiveness of Allah. (3)

اَللّٰهُمَّ صَلِّ عَلَى سَيِّدِنَا مُحَمَّدٍ عَبْدِكَ وَرَسُولِكَ النَّبِيِّ الْأُمِّيِّ
وَعَلَى آلِهِ وَصَحْبِهِ وَسَلِّمْ. (ثلاثا)

O Allah pour blessings upon our master Muhammad, Your slave and
Messenger, the unlettered Prophet, and upon his Family and Companions
and grant them peace. (3)

لَا إِلٰهَ إِلَّا اللهُ وَحْدَهُ لَا شَرِيكَ لَهُ. لَهُ الْمُلْكُ وَلَهُ الْحَمْدُ.
وَهُوَ عَلَى كُلِّ شَيْءٍ قَدِيرٌ. (ثلاثا)

There is no god except Allah alone, without partner. His is the kingdom,
all praise belongs to Him and He is Powerful over all things. (3)

سُبْحَانَ اللهِ وَالْحَمْدُ لِلّٰهِ وَلَا إِلٰهَ إِلَّا اللهُ وَاللهُ أَكْبَرُ.
وَلَا حَوْلَ وَلَا قُوَّةَ إِلَّا بِاللهِ الْعَلِيِّ الْعَظِيمِ. (ثلاثا)

Glory be to Allah and all praise belongs to Allah, there is no god except
Allah, Allah is greater! There is no power and no strength but by Allah,
the High, the Vast. (3)

سُبْحَانَ اللهِ وَبِحَمْدِهِ سُبْحَانَ اللهِ الْعَظِيمِ. (ثلاثا)

Glory be to Allah by His praise, glory be to Allah the Vast. (3)

اَلْحَمْدُ لِلَّهِ وَالشُّكْرُ لِلَّهِ. (ثلاثا)

Praise is due to Allah and thanks be to Allah. (3)

لَقَدْ جَاءَكُمْ رَسُولٌ مِّنْ أَنْفُسِكُمْ عَزِيزٌ عَلَيْهِ مَا عَنِتُمْ. حَرِيصٌ عَلَيْكُمْ. بِالْمُؤْمِنِينَ رَءُوفٌ رَّحِيمٌ.

A Messenger has come to you from among yourselves; your suffering is
distressing to him; he is deeply concerned for you;
he is gentle and merciful to the muminun.

فَإِنْ تَوَلَّوْا فَقُلْ حَسْبِيَ اللَّهُ. لَا إِلَهَ إِلَّا هُوَ. عَلَيْهِ تَوَكَّلْتُ.
وَهُوَ رَبُّ الْعَرْشِ الْعَظِيمِ. (ثلاثا)

But if they turn away, say, "Allah is enough for me. There is no god but
Him. I have put my trust in Him. He is the Lord of the Mighty Throne." (3)

بِسْمِ اللَّهِ الرَّحْمَٰنِ الرَّحِيمِ قُلْ هُوَ اللَّهُ أَحَدٌ. اللَّهُ الصَّمَدُ.
لَمْ يَلِدْ وَلَمْ يُولَدْ. وَلَمْ يَكُنْ لَّهُ كُفُوًا أَحَدٌ. (ثلاثا)

In the name of Allah, All-Merciful, Most Merciful, say: "He is Allah,
Absolute Oneness. Allah, the Everlasting Sustainer of all. He has not
given birth and was not born. And no one is comparable to Him." (3)

تَبَّرَكَ اللَّهُ. (ثلاثا)

Blessed is Allah. (3)

بِسْمِ اللهِ الرَّحْمَنِ الرَّحِيمِ الْحَمْدُ لِلَّهِ رَبِّ الْعَلَمِينَ
الرَّحْمَنِ الرَّحِيمِ مَلِكِ يَوْمِ الدِّينِ. إِيَّاكَ نَعْبُدُ وَإِيَّاكَ نَسْتَعِينُ.
اِهْدِنَا الصِّرَاطَ الْمُسْتَقِيمَ صِرَاطَ الَّذِينَ أَنْعَمْتَ عَلَيْهِمْ
غَيْرِ الْمَغْضُوبِ عَلَيْهِمْ وَلَا الضَّالِّينَ. ءَامِين. (ثلاثا)

In the name of Allah, the All-Merciful, the Most Merciful,
praise be to Allah, the Lord of all the worlds, the All-Merciful,
the Most Merciful, the King of the Day of Judgment. You alone we
worship, You alone we ask for help. Guide us on the Straight Path, the
Path of those whom You have blessed. Not of those with anger upon
them, nor the misguided. Amin. (3)

سُبْحَانَ رَبِّكَ رَبِّ الْعِزَّةِ عَمَّا يَصِفُونَ. وَسَلَامٌ عَلَى الْمُرْسَلِينَ.
وَالْحَمْدُ لِلَّهِ رَبِّ الْعَلَمِينَ.

Glory be to your Lord, the Lord of might, above all else that they
describe. And peace be upon the Messengers. And all praise belongs to
Allah, the Lord of all the worlds.

اَللّٰهُمَّ صَلِّ عَلَى سَيِّدِنَا مُحَمَّدٍ عَبْدِكَ وَنَبِيِّكَ وَرَسُولِكَ النَّبِيِّ
الأُمِّيِّ وَعَلَى ءَالِهِ وَصَحْبِهِ وَسَلِّمْ تَسْلِيمًا. بِقَدْرِ عَظَمَةِ ذَاتِكَ
فِي كُلِّ وَقْتٍ وَحِينَ. (ثلاثا) ءَامِين (ثلاثا)

O Allah pour blessings upon our master Muhammad, Your slave,
Your Messenger, the unlettered Prophet, and upon his Family and

Companions and grant them perfect peace, by the measure of the sublimity of Your Essence at every time and in every age. (3) Amin. (3)

سُبْحَانَ رَبِّكَ رَبِّ الْعِزَّةِ عَمَّا يَصِفُونَ. وَسَلَامٌ عَلَى الْمُرْسَلِينَ. وَالْحَمْدُ لِلَّهِ رَبِّ الْعَالَمِينَ.

Glory be to your Lord, the Lord of might, above all else that they describe. And peace be upon the Messengers. And all praise belongs to Allah, the Lord of all the worlds.

اَللَّهُمَّ إِنِّي أَسْأَلُكَ إِسْلَامًا صَحِيحًا يَصْحَبُهُ الِاسْتِسْلَامُ لِأَوَامِرِكَ وَنَوَاهِيكَ.

O Allah! I ask You for sound Islam
accompanied by submission to Your orders and prohibitions;

وَإِيمَانًا خَالِصًا رَاسِخًا ثَابِتًا مَحْفُوظًا مِنْ جَمِيعِ الشُّبَهِ وَالْمَهَالِكِ.

and for pure Iman, firmly established, enduring,
protected from all ambiguities and dangers;

وَإِحْسَانًا يَزُجُّ بِنَا فِي حَضَرَاتِ الْغُيُوبِ.

and for Ihsan that will drive us into the presence of the Unseen,

وَنَتَطَهَّرُ بِهِ مِنْ أَنْوَاعِ الْغَفَلَاتِ وَسَائِرِ الْعُيُوبِ.

and by which we will be purified from every kind of negligence
and all other defects;

وَإِيقَانَا يَكْشِفُ لَنَا عَنْ حَضَرَاتِ الاَسْمَاءِ وَالصِّفَاتِ.

and a certainty which will reveal to us the presences
of the Names and the Attributes,

وَيَرْحَلُ بِنَا إِلَىٰ مُشَاهَدَةِ أَنْوَارِ تَجَلِّيَاتِ الذَّاتِ.

and by which we will be carried into witnessing
the lights of the Manifestations of the Essence;

وَعِلْمًا نَافِعًا نَفْقَهُ بِهِ كَيْفَ نَتَأَدَّبُ مَعَكَ
وَنُنَاجِيكَ فِي الصَّلَوَاتِ.

and for useful knowledge by which we may understand how to conduct
ourselves in Your presence and how to confide in You in the prayers.

وَامْلَأْ قُلُوبَنَا بِأَنْوَارِ مَعْرِفَتِكَ حَتَّى نَشْهَدَ قَيُّومِيَّتَكَ السَّارِيَةَ
فِي جَمِيعِ الْمَخْلُوقَاتِ.

Fill our hearts with the lights of Your Ma'rifa so that we may witness
Your All-Sustaining Gatheredness that flows in all created things.

وَاجْعَلْنَا مِنْ أَهْلِ دَائِرَةِ الْفَضْلِ الْمَحْبُوبِينَ لَدَيْكَ.

Let us be among the circle of Your bounty, beloved to You.

وَمِنَ الرَّاسِخِينَ الْمُتَمَكِّنِينَ فِي التَّوَكُّلِ

وَصِدْقِ الْاِعْتِمَادِ عَلَيْكَ.

And among the firmly grounded and enduring in reliance
and sincerity of dependence on You.

وَحَقِّقْ رَجَاءَنَا بِالاِجَابَةِ يَا كَرِيمُ يَا وَهَّابُ

فِي كُلِّ مَا سَأَلْنَاكَ.

Realise our hope with the answer, O Generous, O Giving,
in all that we ask You.

وَلَا تَكِلْنَا يَا مَوْلَانَا فِي جَمِيعِ حَرَكَاتِنَا وَسَكَنَاتِنَا

إِلَى أَحَدٍ سِوَاكَ.

Do not entrust us, O Master, in all our movements and stillness,
to anyone other than You.

فَإِنَّكَ عَوَّدْتَنَا إِحْسَانَكَ مِنْ قَبْلِ سُؤَالِنَا

وَنَحْنُ فِي بُطُونِ الْأُمَّهَاتِ.

For You have accustomed us to Your Ihsan before we even asked for it
while we were in our mothers' wombs.

وَرَبَّيْتَنَا بِلَطِيفِ رُبُوبِيَّتِكَ تَرْبِيَةً

تَقْصُرُ عَنْ إِدْرَاكِهَا الْعُقُولُ الْمُنَوَّرَاتُ.

You have raised us with the Gentleness of Your Lordship over existence
in a manner far beyond the perception of illuminated intellects.

فَنَسْأَلُكَ اللَّهُمَّ بِنَبِيِّكَ الَّذِي فَضَّلْتَهُ

عَلَىٰ سَآئِرِ الْأَنْبِيَآءِ وَالْمُرْسَلِينَ.

We ask You, O Allah, by Your Prophet, whom You have preferred
above all other Prophets and Messengers,

وَبِرَسُولِكَ الَّذِي جَعَلْتَ رِسَالَتَهُ عَامَّةً وَرَحْمَةً لِلْخَلَائِقِ أَجْمَعِينَ.

and by Your Messenger whose message You made universal
and a mercy to all creation,

أَنْ تُصَلِّيَ وَتُسَلِّمَ عَلَيْهِ وَعَلَىٰ ءَالِهِ صَلَاةً وَسَلَامًا نَنَالُ بِهِمَا مَحَبَّتَهُ

وَمُتَابَعَتَهُ فِي الْأَقْوَالِ وَالْأَفْعَالِ وَالْمُرَاقَبَةِ وَالْمُشَاهَدَةِ وَالْآدَابِ

وَالْأَخْلَاقِ وَالْأَحْوَالِ.

to bless him and his family and grant them a peace by which we may
attain his love and follow him in words, in deeds, in watching, in
witnessing, in adab, in character and states.

وَنَسْأَلُكَ يَا مَوْلَانَا بِجَاهِهِ أَنْ تَهَبَ لَنَا عِلْمًا نَافِعًا
يَنْتَفِعُ بِهِ كُلُّ سَامِعٍ.

We ask You, O Master, by his rank, to grant us useful knowledge by
which every listener may profit,

وَتَخْشَعُ لَهُ الْقُلُوبُ وَتَقْشَعِرُّ مِنْهُ الْجُلُودُ وَتَجْرِي لَهُ الْمَدَامِعُ.

and every heart may be made humble, and at which the skin may
tremble and tears flow.

إِنَّكَ أَنْتَ الْقَادِرُ الْمُرِيدُ الْعَالِمُ الْحَيُّ الْوَاسِعُ.

You are the All-Powerful, the One who wills,
the Knowing, the Living, the Vast.

سُبْحَانَ رَبِّكَ رَبِّ الْعِزَّةِ عَمَّا يَصِفُونَ. وَسَلَامٌ عَلَى الْمُرْسَلِينَ.
وَالْحَمْدُ لِلَّهِ رَبِّ الْعَالَمِينَ.

Glory be to your Lord, the Lord of might, above all else that they
describe. And peace be upon the Messengers. And all praise belongs to
Allah, the Lord of all the worlds.

ثُمَّ تُصَلِّي بِهَذِهِ الصَّلَاةِ الْمُسَمَّاةِ بِكَنْزِ الْحَقَائِقِ فِي الصَّلَاةِ عَلَى أَشْرَفِ الْخَلَائِقِ الَّتِي تَلَقَّاهَا شَيْخُنَا عَنِ الْمُصْطَفَى صَلَّى اللهُ عَلَهِ وَسَلَّمَ وَهِيَ.

Then you pray the prayer called the Treasury of Truths asking for blessings on the most noble of creatures, which our Shaykh received from the Chosen One, may Allah bless him and grant him peace.

اَللّهُمَّ صَلِّ وَسَلِّمْ بِأَنْوَاعِ كَمَالَاتِكَ فِي جَمِيعِ تَجَلِّيَاتِكَ
عَلَى سَيِّدِنَا وَمَوْلَانَا مُحَمَّدٍ
أَوَّلِ الْأَنْوَارِ الْفَائِضَةِ مِنْ بُحُورِ عَظَمَةِ الذَّاتِ.

O Allah bless and grant peace with every one of Your perfections in all Your manifestations upon our lord and master Muhammad, the first of the lights emanating from the oceans of the sublimity of the Essence,

اَلْمُتَحَقِّقِ فِي عَالَمَيِ الْبُطُونِ وَالظُّهُورِ
بِمَعَانِي الْأَسْمَاءِ وَالصِّفَاتِ.

who realised in the two worlds – the hidden and the seen – the meanings of the Names and the Attributes.

فَهُوَ أَوَّلُ حَامِدٍ وَمُتَعَبِّدٍ بِأَنْوَاعِ الْعِبَادَاتِ وَالْقُرُبَاتِ.

He is the first to give praise and worship with every kind of adoration and good action.

وَالْمُمِدُّ فِي عَالَمَيِ الْأَرْوَاحِ وَالْأَشْبَاحِ بِجَمِيعِ الْمَوْجُودَاتِ.

He is the helper of all created beings
in the world of spirits and the world of forms.

وَعَلَىٰ ءَالِهِ وَأَصْحَابِهِ صَلَاةً تَكْشِفُ لَنَا النِّقَابَ

عَنْ وَجْهِهِ الْكَرِيمِ فِي الْمَرَآئِي وَالْيَقَظَاتِ.

And blessings be upon his family and Companions with a blessing
that will lift the veil from his noble face for us
in visions and in the waking state,

وَتُعَرِّفُنَا بِكَ وَبِهِ فِي جَمِيعِ الْمَرَاتِبِ وَالْحَضَرَاتِ.

and will acquaint us with You and with him
in all ranks and presences.

وَالْطُفْ بِنَا يَا مَوْلَانَا بِجَاهِهِ

فِي الْحَرَكَاتِ وَالسَّكَنَاتِ وَاللَّحَظَاتِ وَالْخَطَرَاتِ. (ثلاثا)

Be gracious to us, O Mawlana, by his rank,
in movements and in stillness, in looks and in thoughts. (3)

سُبْحَانَ رَبِّكَ رَبِّ الْعِزَّةِ عَمَّا يَصِفُونَ. وَسَلَامٌ عَلَى الْمُرْسَلِينَ.

وَالْحَمْدُ لِلَّهِ رَبِّ الْعَالَمِينَ.

Glory be to your Lord, the Lord of might, above all else that they
describe. And peace be upon the Messengers. And all praise belongs to
Allah, the Lord of all the worlds.

أَعُوذُ بِاللهِ مِنَ الشَّيْطَانِ الرَّجِيمِ.

I seek refuge with Allah from the accursed Shaytan:

اَلَّذِينَ قَالَ لَهُمُ النَّاسُ إِنَّ النَّاسَ قَدْ جَمَعُوا لَكُمْ
فَاخْشَوْهُمْ فَزَادَهُمْ إِيمَانًا وَقَالُوا

Those to whom people said,
'The people have gathered against you, so fear them,'
but that merely increased their Iman and they said:

حَسْبُنَا اللهُ وَنِعْمَ الْوَكِيلُ. (عشرا)

"Allah is enough for us and the best of Guardians." (10)

فَانْقَلَبُوا بِنِعْمَةٍ مِنَ اللهِ وَفَضْلٍ لَمْ يَمْسَسْهُمْ سُوءٌ (ثلاثا)

So they returned with blessings from Allah
and with bounty, and no evil touched them. (3)

وَاتَّبَعُوا رِضْوَانَ اللهِ. وَاللهُ ذُو فَضْلٍ عَظِيمٍ. (ثلاثا)

They pursued the pleasure of Allah.
Allah's favour is indeed immense. (3)

وَإِنْ يُرِيدُوا أَنْ يَخْدَعُوكَ فَإِنَّ حَسْبَكَ اللهُ.

And if they intend to deceive you, Allah is enough for you.

هُوَ الَّذِي أَيَّدَكَ بِنَصْرِهِ وَبِالْمُؤْمِنِينَ وَأَلَّفَ بَيْنَ قُلُوبِهِمْ.

It is He Who supported you with His help,
and with the muminun, and unified their hearts.

لَوْ أَنْفَقْتَ مَا فِي الْأَرْضِ جَمِيعًا مَّا أَلَّفْتَ بَيْنَ قُلُوبِهِمْ.

Even if you had spent everything on the earth,
you could not have unified their hearts.

وَلَكِنَّ اللهَ أَلَّفَ بَيْنَهُمْ. إِنَّهُ عَزِيزٌ حَكِيمٌ.

But Allah has unified them. He is the Almighty, All-Wise.

يَـٰٓأَيُّهَا النَّبِيُّ حَسْبُكَ اللهُ. وَمَنِ اتَّبَعَكَ مِنَ الْمُؤْمِنِينَ. (ثلاثا)

O Prophet! Allah is enough for you,
and for the muminun who follow you. (3)

أَلَا يَا لَطِيفُ يَا لَطِيفُ لَكَ اللُّطْفُ

O Gentle, O Knower of subtleties, gentleness is Yours!

فَأَنْتَ اللَّطِيفُ مِنْكَ يَشْمَلُنَا اللُّطْفُ

You are the Gentle, and from You gentleness engulfs us.

لَطِيفُ لَطِيفُ إِنَّنِي مُتَوَسِّلٌ

Latif, Latif, I seek nearness to You

بِلُطْفِكَ فَالْطُفْ بِي وَقَدْ نَزَلَ اللُّطْفُ

by means of Your lutf – be latif to me – and lutf has descended!

بِلُطْفِكَ عُذْنَا يَا لَطِيفُ وَهَا نَحْنُ

Ya Latif, we have sought refuge in Your lutf – we have

دَخَلْنَا فِي وَسْطِ اللُّطْفِ وَانْسَدَلَ اللُّطْفُ

gone into the centre of lutf – and lutf has come down.

نَجَوْنَا بِلُطْفِ اللهِ ذِي اللُّطْفِ إِنَّهُ

We have been freed by the lutf of Allah, the Possessor of lutf,

لَطِيفٌ لَطِيفٌ لُطْفُهُ دَائِمًا لُطْفُ

He is Latif, Latif, His lutf is always that.

أَلَا يَا حَفِيظُ يَا حَفِيظُ لَكَ الْحِفْظُ

O Preserver, O Guardian, guardianship is Yours!

فَأَنْتَ الْحَفِيظُ مِنْكَ يَشْمَلُنَا الْحِفْظُ

You are the Preserver, and from You guardianship engulfs us.

حَفِيظٌ حَفِيظٌ إِنَّا نَتَوَسَّلُ

Hafidh, Hafidh, We seek nearness to You

بِحِفْظِكَ فَاحْفَظْنَا وَقَدْ نَزَلَ الْحِفْظُ

by means of Your hifdh – be hafidh to us – and hifdh has descended.

بِحِفْظِكَ عُذْنَا يَا حَفِيظُ وَهَا نَحْنُ

Ya Hafidh, we have sought refuge in Your hifdh – we have

دَخَلْنَا فِي وَسْطِ الْحِفْظِ وَانْسَدَلَ الْحِفْظُ

gone into the centre of hifdh – and hifdh has come down.

نَجَوْنَا بِحِفْظِ اللهِ ذِي الْحِفْظِ إِنَّهُ

We have been freed by the hifdh of Allah, the Possessor of hifdh.

حَفِيظٌ حَفِيظٌ حِفْظُهُ دَائِمًا حَفْظُ

He is Hafidh, Hafidh, His hifdh is always that.

بِجَاهِ إِمَامِ الْمُرْسَلِينَ مُحَمَّدٍ

By the rank of the Imam of the Messengers, Muhammad,

فَلَوْ لَاهُ عَيْنُ الْحِفْظِ مَا نَزَلَ الْحِفْظُ

If it were not for him, the source of hifdh,
hifdh would not have descended.

عَلَيْهِ صَلَاةُ اللهِ مَا قَالَ مُنْشِدُ

Blessings be upon him as long as there is one who chants:

أَلَا يَا حَفِيظُ يَا حَفِيظُ لَكَ الْحِفْظُ

Ya Hafidh, ya Hafidh, the hifdh is Yours!

لَاۤ إِلَهَ إِلَّا اللهُ. (عَشْرَا)

No god – except Allah (10)

لَاۤ إِلَهَ إِلَّا اللهُ. سَيِّدُنَا مُحَمَّدٌ رَسُولُ اللهِ.

No god – except Allah;
our master Muhammad is the Messenger of Allah.

صَلَّى اللهُ عَلَيْهِ وَسَلَّمَ وَعَلَىٰ ءَالِهِ.

May Allah bless him and his family and grant them peace.

ثَبِّتْنَا يَا رَبِّ بِقَوْلِهَا. وَانْفَعْنَا يَا مَوْلَانَا بِذِكْرِهَا.

O Lord, make us firm by its recital.
O Mawlana, give us benefit from its invocation.

وَأَدْخِلْنَا فِي مَيْدَانِ حِصْنِهَا. وَاجْعَلْنَا مِنْ أَفْرَادِ أَهْلِهَا.

Let us enter into the fortress of its protection.
And let us be among its people,

وَعِنْدَ الْمَوْتِ نَاطِقِينَ بِهَا. عَالِمِينَ بِهَا.

who at the time of death say it, having knowledge of what is in it.

وَاحْشُرْنَا فِي زُمْرَةِ سَيِّدِنَا وَمَوْلَانَا مُحَمَّدٍ صَلَّى اللهُ عَلَيْهِ وَسَلَّمَ
وَعَلَىٰ ءَالِهِ وَأَصْحَابِهِ وَعَلَىٰ جَمِيعِ عِبَادِ اللهِ الْمُؤْمِنِينَ.

Gather us into the company of our lord and master Muhammad, may

Allah pour blessings upon him and grant him peace, and his family and
Companions and all the believing slaves of Allah.

ءَامِين (ثلاثا)

Amin. (3)

وَسَلَامٌ عَلَى الاَنْبِيَآءِ وَالْمُرْسَلِينَ ۰ (ثلاثا)

And peace be upon the Prophets and the Messengers. (3)

وَعَلَىٰ جَمِيعِ عِبَادِ اللهِ الصَّالِحِينَ۰

And on all the Right-acting slaves of Allah (Saliheen).

وَءَاخِرُ دَعْوَانَآ أَنِ الْحَمْدُ لِلَّهِ رَبِّ الْعَٰلَمِينَ۰

The end of our call is: Praise be to Allah, the Lord of the worlds.

وَلَا حَوْلَ وَلَا قُوَّةَ إِلَّا بِاللهِ الْعَلِيّ الْعَظِيمِ۰

There is no power and no strength but by Allah,
the High, the Vast.

وَمَا تَوْفِيقِيَ إِلَّا بِاللهِ۰ عَلَيْهِ تَوَكَّلْتُ۰ وَإِلَيْهِ أُنِيبُ۰

My success is only by Allah. In Him I have put my trust.
And to Him I turn in renewal.

وَالْحَمْدُ لِلَّهِ عَلَىٰ نِعْمَةِ الاِسْلَامِ وَكَفَىٰ بِهَا نِعْمَةً۰

Praise belongs to Allah for the blessing of Islam,
and it is blessing enough.

وإن وفقك الله إلى إكثار من لا إله إلا الله فعلى رأس كل مائة تقول سيدنا
محمد رسول الله صلى الله عليه وسلم الخ ... كما سبق

*And if Allah gives you success in doing more of la ilaha illa'llah then at the
end of every hundred you should say our master Muhammad is the Messenger of
Allah, may Allah bless him and his family and grant them peace.*

يَآ أَوَّلُ يَآ ءَاخِرُ يَا ظَاهِرُ يَا بَاطِنُ. اِسْمَعْ نِدَاۤئِي بِمَا سَمِعْتَ بِهِ نِدَاۤءَ

O First! O Last! O Manifest! O Hidden!

Hear my cry as you heard the cry

عَبْدِكَ سَيِّدِنَا زَكَرِيَّاۤءَ عَلَيْهِ السَّلَامُ.

of Your slave, our master Zakariyya', peace be upon him.

وَانْصُرْنِي بِكَ لَكَ.

Give me victory by You – for You.

وَأَيِّدْنِي بِكَ لَكَ.

Support me by You – for You.

وَاجْمَعْ بَيْنِي وَبَيْنَكَ.

Join me to You.

وَحُلْ بَيْنِي وَبَيْنَ غَيْرِكَ.

Separate me from other-than-You.

الله (عشرا)

Allah (10)

وإن أردت الزيادة من ذكر الاسم المفرد في غير الورد فلك ذلك ، ومن زاد
زاده الله، وقد ذكر العارفون بالله للاسم المفرد فوائد لا تعد ولا تحصى

If you want to do more of the dhikr of the Unique Name outside of the Wird you
may do so, and whoever does more, Allah will give more, and the 'arifun of Allah
have mentioned innumerable benefits from the Unique Name.

The Lesser Wird

بِسْمِ اللهِ الرَّحْمٰنِ الرَّحِيمِ.

In the name of Allah, All-Merciful, Most Merciful.

اَللّٰهُمَّ إِنِّي أَسْأَلُكَ بِسِرِّ الذَّاتِ.

O Allah, I ask You by the secret of the Essence.

وَبِذَاتِ السِّرِّ. هُوَ أَنْتَ وَأَنْتَ هُوَ.

And by the Essence of the secret. He is You and You are He.

اِحْتَجَبْتُ بِنُورِ اللهِ. وَبِنُورِ عَرْشِ اللهِ.

I have veiled myself with the light of Allah,
and by the light of the Throne of Allah,

وَبِكُلِّ إِسْمِ اللهِ مِنْ عَدُوِّي وَعَدُوِّ اللهِ.

and with all the Names of Allah from my enemy
and the enemy of Allah.

بِمِائَةِ أَلْفٍ لَا حَوْلَ وَلَا قُوَّةَ إِلَّا بِاللهِ.

With one hundred thousand "there is no power
and no strength but by Allah."

خَتَمْتُ عَلَى نَفْسِي وَعَلَى دِينِي وَعَلَى كُلِّ شَيْءٍ أَعْطَانِيهِ رَبِّي.

I have set a seal upon my self and my Deen
and upon everything given to me by my Lord.

بِخَاتِمِ اللهِ الْمَنِيعِ الَّذِي

خَتَمَ بِهِ أَقْطَارَ السَّمَوَاتِ وَالْأَرْضِ.

With the protecting seal of Allah
with which He has sealed the heavens and the earth.

وَحَسْبُنَا اللهُ وَنِعْمَ الْوَكِيلُ. نِعْمَ الْمَوْلَى وَنِعْمَ النَّصِيرُ.

Allah is enough for us and He is the best Guardian.
The best Protector, the best Helper.

وَصَلَّى اللهُ عَلَى سَيِّدِنَا وَمَوْلَانَا مُحَمَّدٍ

The blessings of Allah be upon our lord and master Muhammad,

وَعَلَى آلِهِ وَأَصْحَابِهِ أَجْمَعِينَ.

and upon all his family and Companions.

وَسَلَّمَ تَسْلِيمًا كَثِيرًا.

And grant them great peace.

وَالْحَمْدُ لِلَّهِ رَبِّ الْعَالَمِينَ.

Praise belongs to Allah, the Lord of the worlds.

20

ثم تقول الدعاء المبارك وهو:

Then you may say this blessed du'a

يَا وَدُودُ. (ثلاثا)

O Lover! (3)

يَا ذَا الْعَرْشِ الْمَجِيدِ. (ثلاثا)

O Possessor of the glorious Throne! (3)

يَا مُبْدِئُ يَا مُعِيدُ. (ثلاثا)

O You Who Originate, O You Who Bring back to life! (3)

يَا فَعَّالًا لِمَا يُرِيدُ. (ثلاثا)

O He Who does whatever He wills! (3)

أَسْأَلُكَ بِنُورِ وَجْهِكَ الَّذِي مَلَأَ أَرْكَانَ عَرْشِكَ. (ثلاثا)

I ask You by the light of Your face
that fills every corner of Your Throne, (3)

وَأَسْأَلُكَ بِالْقُدْرَةِ الَّتِي قَدَرْتَ بِهَا عَلَى خَلْقِكَ. (ثلاثا)

and I ask You by the power You exercise over Your creation, (3)

وَبِرَحْمَتِكَ الَّتِي وَسِعَتْ كُلَّ شَيْءٍ. (ثلاثا)

and by Your mercy that encompasses all things: (3)

لَا إِلَهَ إِلَّا أَنْتَ يَا مُغِيثُ أَغِثْنَا. (ثلاثا)

No god but You – O Rescuer – rescue us! (3)

سُبْحَانَ رَبِّكَ رَبِّ الْعِزَّةِ عَمَّا يَصِفُونَ. وَسَلَامٌ عَلَى الْمُرْسَلِينَ. وَالْحَمْدُ لِلَّهِ رَبِّ الْعَالَمِينَ.

Glory be to your Lord, the Lord of might, above all else that they describe. And peace be upon the Messengers. And all praise belongs to Allah, the Lord of all the worlds.

اَللَّهُ لَطِيفٌ بِعِبَادِهِ. يَرْزُقُ مَنْ يَشَاءُ. وَهُوَ الْقَوِيُّ الْعَزِيزُ. (تسعا)

Allah is gentle with His slaves. He provides for anyone He wills, and He is the Most Strong, the Almighty. (9)

سُبْحَانَ رَبِّكَ رَبِّ الْعِزَّةِ عَمَّا يَصِفُونَ. وَسَلَامٌ عَلَى الْمُرْسَلِينَ. وَالْحَمْدُ لِلَّهِ رَبِّ الْعَالَمِينَ. ○

Glory be to your Lord, the Lord of might, above all else that they describe. And peace be upon the Messengers. And all praise belongs to Allah, the Lord of all the worlds.

وعند الصباح تزيد:

At Subh you add:

22

لَا إِلَهَ إِلَّا اللهُ وَاللهُ أَكْبَرُ. وَسُبْحَانَ اللهِ وَبِحَمْدِهِ وَأَسْتَغْفِرُ
اللهَ. وَلَا حَوْلَ وَلَا قُوَّةَ إِلَّا بِاللهِ. هُوَ الْاوَّلُ وَالْآخِرُ وَالظَّاهِرُ
وَالْبَاطِنُ. بِيَدِهِ الْخَيْرُ. يُحْيِي وَيُمِيتُ.
وَهُوَ عَلَى كُلِّ شَيْءٍ قَدِيرٌ. (عشرا)

There is no god except Allah and Allah is greater. Glory be to Allah
and by His praise, and I seek forgiveness from Allah. And there is no
power and no strength but by Allah. He is the First and the Last and the
Outwardly Manifest and the Inwardly Hidden. Good is in His hand, He
makes to live and makes to die, and He is powerful over all things. (10)

وَصَلَّى اللهُ عَلَى سَيِّدِنَا وَمَوْلَانَا مُحَمَّدٍ وَعَلَى ءَالِهِ وَصَحْبِهِ وَسَلَّمَ
تَسْلِيمًا. عَدَدَ خَلْقِكَ وَرِضَا نَفْسِكَ وَزِنَةَ عَرْشِكَ
وَمِدَادَ كَلِمَاتِكَ.

And blessings of Allah upon our lord and master, Muhammad, and upon
his family and Companions and grant them perfect peace – as great as
the number of Your creations and Your pleasure and the weight of Your
Throne and the ink of Your words.

سُبْحَانَ رَبِّكَ رَبِّ الْعِزَّةِ عَمَّا يَصِفُونَ. وَسَلَامٌ عَلَى الْمُرْسَلِينَ.
وَالْحَمْدُ لِلَّهِ رَبِّ الْعَلَمِينَ.

Glory be to your Lord, the Lord of might, above all else that they
describe. And peace be upon the Messengers. And all praise belongs to
Allah, the Lord of all the worlds.

سُبْحَانَ اللهِ وَالْحَمْدُ لِلَّهِ وَلَا إِلَهَ إِلَّا اللهُ وَاللهُ أَكْبَرُ.

وَلَا حَوْلَ وَلَا قُوَّةَ إِلَّا بِاللهِ الْعَلِيِّ الْعَظِيمِ. عَدَدَ مَا عَلِمَ

وَزِنَةَ مَا عَلِمَ وَمِلَا مَا عَلِمَ. (ثلاثا)

Glory be to Allah and praise be to Allah and there is no god except Allah and Allah is greater. There is no power and no strength but by Allah, the High, the Vast, in quantity as great as what He knows, in weight as much as He knows and in volume as much as He knows. (3)

سُبْحَانَ رَبِّكَ رَبِّ الْعِزَّةِ عَمَّا يَصِفُونَ. وَسَلَامٌ عَلَى الْمُرْسَلِينَ.

وَالْحَمْدُ لِلَّهِ رَبِّ الْعَالَمِينَ ۞

Glory be to your Lord, the Lord of might, above all else that they describe. And peace be upon the Messengers. And all praise belongs to Allah, the Lord of all the worlds.

The Seal of The Wird

أدعية ختام الورد

اللّٰهُمَّ افْتَحْ بِصَآئِرَنَا لِمُرَاقَبَتِكَ وَمُشَاهَدَتِكَ بِجُودِكَ وَفَضْلِكَ.

O Allah, open our inner sight for us to watch You and witness You by Your generosity and overflowing.

وَنَوِّرْ سَرَآئِرَنَا لِتَجَلِّيَاتِ أَسْمَآئِكَ وَصِفَاتِكَ بِحِلْمِكَ وَكَرَمِكَ.

And illuminate our secret to the manifestations of Your Names and Attributes through Your forbearance and noble generosity.

وَأَفْنِنَا عَنْ وُجُودِنَا الْمَجَازِي

فِي وُجُودِكَ الْحَقِيقِي بِطَوْلِكَ وَمِنَّكَ.

And annihilate us from our metaphorical existence
in Your real existence, by Your favour and gifts.

وَأَبْقِنَا بِكَ لَا بِنَا مُحَافِظِينَ عَلَى شَرِيعَتِكَ وَسُنَّةِ نَبِيِّكَ.

And make us continue by You, not by us, preserving Your Shari'a
and the Sunna of Your Prophet.

إِنَّكَ عَلَى كُلِّ شَيْءٍ قَدِيرٌ. وَبِالإِجَابَةِ جَدِيرٌ.

You are powerful over all things – and are disposed to answer.

بِسِرِّ وَبَرَكَةِ بِسْمِ اللهِ الرَّحْمَنِ الرَّحِيمِ الْحَمْدُ لِلَّهِ رَبِّ الْعَلَمِينَ
الرَّحْمَنِ الرَّحِيمِ مَلِكِ يَوْمِ الدِّينِ. إِيَّاكَ نَعْبُدُ وَإِيَّاكَ نَسْتَعِينُ. اهْدِنَا
الصِّرَاطَ الْمُسْتَقِيمَ صِرَاطَ الَّذِينَ أَنْعَمْتَ عَلَيْهِمْ غَيْرِ الْمَغْضُوبِ
عَلَيْهِمْ وَلَا الضَّالِّينَ. ءَامِين.

By the secret and the blessing of: In the name of Allah, All-Merciful,
the Most Merciful. Praise be to Allah, Lord of the worlds, the All-
Merciful, the Most Merciful, the King of the Day of Judgment. You
alone we worship, You alone we ask for help. Guide us on the Straight
Path, the Path of those whom You have blessed, not of those with anger
upon them, nor of the misguided. Amin.

سُبْحَانَ رَبِّكَ رَبِّ الْعِزَّةِ عَمَّا يَصِفُونَ. وَسَلَامٌ عَلَى الْمُرْسَلِينَ.
وَالْحَمْدُ لِلَّهِ رَبِّ الْعَلَمِينَ ○

Glory be to your Lord, the Lord of might, above all else that they
describe. And peace be upon the Messengers.
And praise belongs to Allah, the Lord of all the worlds.

ثم تدعو لنفسك ولوالديك ولمشائخك ولشيخ وقتك ولأمير المومنين خصوصا
ولكافة المسلمين عموما

Then pray for yourself and your parents and for your shaykhs and for the Shaykh
of your age and for the Amir al-Muminin in particular
and for all the Muslims in general.

اللَّهُمَّ صَلِّ عَلَى سَيِّدِنَا مُحَمَّدٍ وَعَلَى ءَالِ سَيِّدِنَا مُحَمَّدٍ صَلَاةً تُنْجِينَا
بِهَا مِنْ جَمِيعِ الْأَهْوَالِ وَالآفَاتِ. وَتَقْضِي لَنَا بِهَا جَمِيعَ الْحَاجَاتِ.
وَتُطَهِّرُنَا بِهَا مِنْ جَمِيعِ السَّيِّئَاتِ. وَتَرْفَعُنَا بِهَا
أَعْلَا الدَّرَجَاتِ. وَتَبْلُغُنَا بِهَا أَقْصَى الْغَايَاتِ مِنْ جَمِيعِ الْخَيْرَاتِ
فِي الْحَيَاةِ وَبَعْدَ الْمَمَاتِ.

O Allah, bless our master Muhammad and the family of our master
Muhammad with a blessing by which You will save us from every fear
and harm, and by which You will supply us with all our needs, and by
which You will purify us from all evils, and by which You will raise
us to the highest degrees, and by which You will make us attain the
furthest goal of good in life and after death.

اَللّٰهُمَّ أَنْزِلْ عَلَيْنَا فِي هَذِهِ السَّاعَةِ مِنْ خَيْرِكَ وَبَرَكَاتِكَ.

كَمَا أَنْزَلْتَ عَلَى أَوْلِيَائِكَ. وَخَصَّصْتَ بِهِ أَحِبَّائَكَ. وَأَذِقْنَا بَرْدَ

عَفْوِكَ وَحَلَاوَةَ مَغْفِرَتِكَ. وَانْشُرْ عَلَيْنَا رَحْمَتَكَ الَّتِي وَسِعَتْ كُلَّ

شَيْءٍ. وَارْزُقْنَا مِنْكَ مَحَبَّةً وَقَبُولًا. وَتَوْبَةً نَصُوحًا. وَإِجَابَةً وَمَغْفِرَةً

وَعَافِيَةً. تَعُمُّ الْحَاضِرِينَ وَالْغَائِبِينَ وَالْاَحْيَاءَ وَالْمَيِّتِينَ. بِرَحْمَتِكَ

يَا أَرْحَمَ الرَّاحِمِينَ يَا أَرْحَمَ الرَّاحِمِينَ يَا أَرْحَمَ الرَّاحِمِينَ.

O Allah, in this hour send down some of Your good and Your baraka
on us as You sent it down on Your near ones, and singled it out for Your
lovers. Let us taste the coolness of Your pardon and the sweetness of
Your forgiveness. Spread over us Your compassion which encompasses
all things. Provide us with Your love and acceptance and sincere
turning to You, and Your response to our asking, forgiveness, and wellbeing that will encompass those present and absent,
the living and the dead, by Your mercy,
O Most Merciful of the merciful. (3)

اَللّٰهُمَّ لَا تُخَيِّبْنَا مِمَّا سَأَلْنَاكَ. وَلَا تَحْرِمْنَا مِمَّا رَجَوْنَاكَ. وَاحْفَظْنَا

وَاحْفَظْنَا وَاحْفَظْنَا فِي الْمَحْيَا وَالْمَمَاتِ.

إِنَّكَ مُجِيبُ الدَّعَوَاتِ.

O Allah, do not disappoint us in what we ask of You. Do not deny us
what we hope for from You. Protect us. Protect us. Protect us in life
and in death. You are the Answerer of prayers.

سُبْحَانَ رَبِّكَ رَبِّ الْعِزَّةِ عَمَّا يَصِفُونَ. وَسَلَامٌ عَلَى الْمُرْسَلِينَ.
وَالْحَمْدُ لِلَّهِ رَبِّ الْعَالَمِينَ.

Glory be to your Lord, the Lord of might, above all else that they
describe. And peace be upon the Messengers.
And praise belongs to Allah, the Lord of all the worlds.

اللَّهُمَّ إِنِّي أَسْتَخِيرُكَ بِعِلْمِكَ. وَأَسْتَقْدِرُكَ بِقُدْرَتِكَ.
وَأَسْأَلُكَ مِنْ فَضْلِكَ الْعَظِيمِ الأَعْظَمِ.

O Allah, I ask You to choose by Your knowledge. And I ask You to decree
by Your power. And I ask You for some of Your great and sublime bounty.

فَإِنَّكَ تَقْدِرُ وَلَا أَقْدِرُ. وَتَعْلَمُ وَلَا أَعْلَمُ. وَأَنْتَ عَلَّامُ الْغُيُوبِ.

For You have power and I do not. You know and I do not.
And You are the Knower of the Unseen.

اللَّهُمَّ إِنْ كُنْتَ تَعْلَمُ أَنَّ هَذَا الأَمْرَ وَهُوَ جَمِيعُ حَرَكَاتِي وَسَكَنَاتِي
الظَّاهِرَةَ وَالْبَاطِنَةَ. مِنْ قَوْلٍ وَفِعْلٍ وَخُلُقٍ وَحَالٍ. عِبَادَةً وَعَادَةً.
فِي حَقِّي وَفِي حَقِّ غَيْرِي. فِي هَذَا الْيَوْمِ وَفِيمَا بَعْدَهُ { أَوْ: فِي
هَذِهِ اللَّيْلَةِ وَفِي مَا بَعْدَهَا } وَفِي بَقِيَّةِ عُمُرِي.

O Allah, if You know that this affair – all my movement and stillness,
apparent and hidden, in speech, deeds, character and state, in
spiritual work and daily life, as regards myself and others, in this day
(or night) and those after it, and all the rest of my life –

خَيْرٌ لِّي فِي دِينِي وَدُنْيَايَ وَمَعَاشِي وَمَعَادِي وَعَاقِبَةِ أَمْرِي
وَعَاجِلِهِ وَءَاجِلِهِ. فَاقْدُرْهُ لِي وَيَسِّرْهُ لِي ثُمَّ بَارِكْ لِي فِيهِ.

is good for me in my Deen, and my worldly existence, in this life and
my next life, and my final end, be it sooner or later, then destine it for
me, make it easy for me and bless me in it.

وَإِنْ كُنْتَ تَعْلَمُ أَنَّ هٰذَا الْأَمْرَ وَهُوَ جَمِيعُ حَرَكَاتِي وَسَكَنَاتِي
الظَّاهِرَةِ وَالْبَاطِنَةِ. مِنْ قَوْلٍ وَفِعْلٍ وَخُلُقٍ وَحَالٍ. عِبَادَةً وَعَادَةً.
فِي حَقِّي وَفِي حَقِّ غَيْرِي. فِي هٰذَا الْيَوْمِ وَفِيمَا بَعْدَهُ {أَوْ: فِي
هٰذِهِ اللَّيْلَةِ وَفِي مَا بَعْدَهَا} وَفِي بَقِيَّةِ عُمْرِي.

But if You know that this affair – all my movement and stillness,
apparent and hidden, in speech, deeds, character and state, in spiritual
work and daily life, as regards myself and others, in this day (or night)
and those after it, and all the rest of my life –

شَرٌّ لِّي فِي دِينِي وَدُنْيَايَ وَمَعَاشِي وَمَعَادِي وَعَاقِبَةِ أَمْرِي وَعَاجِلِهِ
وَءَاجِلِهِ. فَاصْرِفْهُ عَنِّي وَاصْرِفْنِي عَنْهُ. وَاقْدُرْ لِي الْخَيْرَ حَيْثُ كَانَ
ثُمَّ رَضِّنِي بِهِ. إِنَّكَ عَلَىٰ كُلِّ شَيْءٍ قَدِيرٌ.

is evil for me in my Deen, and my worldly existence, in this life and my
next life, and my final end, be it sooner or later, then divert it from me
and divert me from it, and destine the good for me wherever it may be
and make me pleased with it. You have power over all things.

اَللَّهُمَّ اقْسِمْ لَنَا مِنْ خَشْيَتِكَ مَا تَحُولُ بِهِ بَيْنَنَا وَبَيْنَ مَعَاصِيكَ.

وَمِنْ طَاعَتِكَ مَا تُبَلِّغُنَا بِهِ جَنَّتَكَ.

وَمِنَ الْيَقِينِ مَا تُهَوِّنُ بِهِ عَلَيْنَا مَصَآئِبَ الدُّنْيَا.

O Allah, provision us with fear of You that may come between us and acts of disobedience against You. And grant us obedience to You that will bring us to Your Garden. And grant us certainty that will make the misfortunes of this world easy for us.

اَللَّهُمَّ مَتِّعْنَا بِأَسْمَاعِنَا وَأَبْصَارِنَا وَقُوَّتِنَا مَآ أَحْيَيْتَنَا. وَاجْعَلْهُ الْوَارِثَ مِنَّا. وَاجْعَلْ ثَارَنَا عَلَى مَنْ ظَلَمَنَا. وَانْصُرْنَا عَلَى مَنْ عَادَانَا. وَلَا تَجْعَلْ مُصِيبَتَنَا فِي دِينِنَا. وَلَا تَجْعَلِ الدُّنْيَا أَكْبَرَ هَمِّنَا. وَلَا مَبْلَغَ عِلْمِنَا. وَلَا غَايَةَ رَغْبَتِنَا. وَلَآ إِلَى النَّارِ مَصِيرَنَا. وَلَا تُسَلِّطْ عَلَيْنَا بِذُنُوبِنَا مَنْ لَا يَرْحَمْنَا.

يَآ أَرْحَمَ الرَّاحِمِينَ. يَآ أَرْحَمَ الرَّاحِمِينَ. يَآ أَرْحَمَ الرَّاحِمِينَ.

O Allah, let us enjoy our hearing and vision and strength for as long as You grant us life and make it our legacy. Avenge us on those who have wronged us and give us victory over those who have attacked us, and do not give us misfortune in our Deen. Do not let this world be the greatest of our cares, nor the scope of our knowledge, nor the object of our desire, and do not let our homecoming be the Fire. Do not place over us because of our wrong actions those who will not show mercy to us. O Most Merciful of the merciful. (3)

اَللَّهُمَّ يَا رَبِّ بِجَاهِ نَبِيِّكَ الْمُصْطَفَىٰ. وَرَسُولِكَ الْمُرْتَضَىٰ. طَهِّرْ
قُلُوبَنَا مِنْ كُلِّ وَصْفٍ يُبَاعِدُنَا عَنْ مُشَاهَدَتِكَ وَمَحَبَّتِكَ. وَأَمِتْنَا
عَلَى السُّنَّةِ وَالْجَمَاعَةِ وَالشَّوْقِ إِلَىٰ لِقَائِكَ يَا ذَا الْجَلَالِ وَالْاِكْرَامِ.
يَا ذَا الْجَلَالِ وَالْاِكْرَامِ. يَا ذَا الْجَلَالِ وَالْاِكْرَامِ.

O Allah! O Lord, by the rank of Your chosen Prophet and approved
Messenger, purify our hearts of every attribute that might separate
us from Your contemplation and love. Let us die in the Sunna and the
Jama'a and in yearning for Your encounter.
O Lord of majesty and generosity. (3)

فَسُبْحَانَ اللهِ حِينَ تُمْسُونَ وَحِينَ تُصْبِحُونَ وَلَهُ الْحَمْدُ فِي السَّمَٰوَٰتِ
وَالْاَرْضِ وَعَشِيًّا وَحِينَ تُظْهِرُونَ. يُخْرِجُ الْحَيَّ مِنَ الْمَيِّتِ وَيُخْرِجُ
الْمَيِّتَ مِنَ الْحَيِّ وَيُحْيِ الْاَرْضَ بَعْدَ مَوْتِهَا. وَكَذَٰلِكَ تُخْرَجُونَ.

Glory be to Allah both in your evening hour and in your morning hour.
Praise belongs to Him in the heavens and the earth, alike at the setting
of the sun and in your noontide hour. He brings forth the living from
the dead and brings forth the dead from the living and brings the earth
to life after it was dead. In that manner you shall be brought forth.

اَللَّهُمَّ إِنَّا نَسْأَلُكَ رِضَاكَ وَالْجَنَّةَ.
وَمَا يُقَرِّبُ إِلَيْهِمَا مِنْ قَوْلٍ وَعَمَلٍ.

O Allah, we ask You for Your pleasure and the Garden,
and the speech and action that bring us near to them.

وَنَعُوذُ بِكَ مِنْ سَخَطِكَ وَالنَّارِ.

وَمَا يُقَرِّبُ إِلَيْهِمَا مِنْ قَوْلٍ وَعَمَلٍ.

And we take refuge with You from Your displeasure and the Fire,
and the speech and action that bring us near to them.

اَللّٰهُمَّ يَا سَابِغَ النِّعَمِ. وَيَا دَافِعَ النِّقَمِ. وَيَا فَارِجَ الْغُمَمِ.

وَيَا كَاشِفَ الظُّلَمِ. وَيَا أَعْدَلَ مَنْ حَكَمَ.

وَيَا حَسْبَ مَنْ ظُلِمَ. وَيَا وَلِيَّ مَنْ ظُلِمَ.

O Allah, O Abundant in blessing. O Repeller of adversities. O One
Who frees us from troubles. O One Who removes the darkness. O
Most Just of those who judge. O Reckoner of those who are unjust.
O Protector of those who are wronged!

يَا أَوَّلًا بِلَا بِدَايَةٍ. يَا آخِرًا بِلَا نِهَايَةٍ. يَا مَنْ لَهُ إِسْمٌ بِلَا كُنْيَةٍ.

فَرِّجْ عَنَّا وَعَنْ جَمِيعِ الْمُسْلِمِينَ مَا هُمْ فِيهِ.

O First without beginning! O Last without end! O You Who have a name
without a kunya! Free us and all the muslims from the state they are in –

بِسِرِّ اسْمِكَ الْمَخْزُونِ الْمَكْنُونِ الْمُبَارَكِ، الطَّاهِرِ الْمُطَهَّرِ الْمُقَدَّسِ.

إِنَّكَ عَلَى كُلِّ شَيْءٍ قَدِيرٌ. وَبِالْاِجَابَةِ جَدِيرٌ.

By the secret of Your Guarded, Hidden, Blessed, Pure, Purified,
Wholly Pure Name. You are able to do all things,
and disposed to answer our prayers.

سُبْحَانَ رَبِّكَ رَبِّ الْعِزَّةِ عَمَّا يَصِفُونَ. وَسَلَامٌ عَلَى الْمُرْسَلِينَ.
وَالْحَمْدُ لِلَّهِ رَبِّ الْعَٰلَمِينَ ۝

Glory be to your Lord, the Lord of might, above all else that they
describe. And peace be upon the Messengers.
And praise belongs to Allah, the Lord of all the worlds.

The Wird of the Salat
أدعية دبر الصلوات

وَبَعْدَ كُلِّ فَرِيضَةٍ مِنَ الصَّلَوَاتِ الخَمْسِ تَقُولُ:

After each of the fard prayers say:

أَسْتَغْفِرُ اللهَ الْعَظِيمَ الَّذِي لَآ إِلَهَ إِلَّا هُوَ الْحَيُّ الْقَيُّومَ
وَأَتُوبُ إِلَيْهِ. (ثلاثا)

I ask forgiveness of Allah the Vast. There is no god but He, the Living,
the Eternal: to Him I turn. (3)

اَللّٰهُمَّ مَغْفِرَتُكَ أَوْسَعُ مِنْ ذُنُوبِي
وَرَحْمَتُكَ أَرْجَىٰ عِنْدِي مِنْ عَمَلِي. (ثلاثا)

O Allah, Your forgiveness is vaster than my wrong actions
and Your mercy more hopeful for me than my behaviour. (3)

اَللّٰهُمَّ صَلِّ عَلَى سَيِّدِنَا مُحَمَّدٍ عَبْدِكَ وَنَبِيِّكَ وَرَسُولِكَ النَّبِيِّ الأُمِّيِّ
وَعَلَىٰ ءَالِهِ وَصَحْبِهِ وَسَلِّمْ تَسْلِيمًا.
بِقَدْرِ عَظَمَةِ ذَاتِكَ فِي كُلِّ وَقْتٍ وَحِينٍ. (ثلاثا)

O Allah, bless our master Muhammad, Your slave, Prophet and
Messenger, the unlettered Prophet and his family and Companions, and

grant them peace, as great in measure as Your essence, at all times and in every age. (3)

اَللّٰهُمَّ إِنَّا نَسْأَلُكَ فِعْلَ الْخَيْرَاتِ وَتَرْكَ الْمُنْكَرَاتِ وَحُبَّ الْمَسَاكِينِ. وَإِذَآ أَرَدْتَ بِعِبَادِكَ فِتْنَةً فَاقْبِضْنَآ إِلَيْكَ غَيْرَ مَفْتُونِينَ. (ثلاثا) ءَامِين. ءَامِين. ءَامِين.

O Allah, we ask You that we should do good, leave what is objectionable and love the poor. If You will that there be schism among Your slaves, grant that You will take us to You uncorrupted. (3) Amin. Amin. Amin.

سُبْحَانَ رَبِّكَ رَبِّ الْعِزَّةِ عَمَّا يَصِفُونَ. وَسَلَامٌ عَلَى الْمُرْسَلِينَ. وَالْحَمْدُ لِلَّهِ رَبِّ الْعَٰلَمِينَ.

Glory be to your Lord, the Lord of might, above all else that they describe. And peace be upon the Messengers.
And praise belongs to Allah, the Lord of all the worlds.

ثُمَّ تُسَبِّحُ اللّٰهَ ثَلَاثًا وَثَلَاثِينَ وَتَحْمَدُهُ كَذَالِكَ وَتُكَبِّرُهُ كَذَالِكَ وَتَخْتِمُ الْمِائَةَ بِـ:

Then say:

سُبْحَانَ اللّٰهِ. (ثلاثا وثلاثين)

Glory be to Allah. (33)

اَلْحَمْدُ لِلَّهِ. (ثلاثا وثلاثين)

Praise belongs to Allah. (33)

اَللّٰهُ أَكْبَرُ. (ثلاثا وثلاثين)

Allah is greater. (33)

Then seal the hundred with:

لَاۤ إِلٰهَ إِلَّا اللّٰهُ وَحْدَهُ لَا شَرِيكَ لَهُ. لَهُ الْمُلْكُ وَلَهُ الْحَمْدُ.
وَهُوَ عَلٰى كُلِّ شَيْءٍ قَدِيرٌ.

There is no god except Allah, alone, without partner. The kingdom and
the praise belong to Him. And He has power over all things.

ثُمَّ تَقُولُ:

Then say:

أَسْتَغْفِرُ اللّٰهَ. (ثلاثا)

I ask forgiveness of Allah. (3)

الْحَمْدُ لِلّٰهِ وَالشُّكْرُ لِلّٰهِ. (ثلاثا)

Praise be to Allah and thanks be to Allah. (3)

لَا حَوْلَ وَلَا قُوَّةَ إِلَّا بِاللّٰهِ.

There is no power and no strength but through Allah.

اَللّٰهُمَّ إِنَّا نَسْتَوْدِعُكَ دِينَنَا وَإِيمَانَنَا فَاحْفَظْهُمَا عَلَيْنَا حِفْظًا مُحَمَّدِيًّا
فِي حَيَاتِنَا وَعِنْدَ مَمَاتِنَا وَبَعْدَ وَفَاتِنَا وَارْزُقْنَا كِلَاهُمَا بِمُتَابَعَتِهِ صَلَّى
اللّٰهُ عَلَيْهِ وَسَلَّمَ فِي الْاَقْوَالِ وَالْاَفْعَالِ وَالْاَخْلَاقِ وَالْاَحْوَالِ

مُرِيدِينَ بِذَ'لِكَ وَجْهَكَ الْكَرِيمَ.

يَا أَكْرَمَ الاَكْرَمِينَ. ءَامِينَ.

O Allah, we commend our Deen and our Iman to You, so protect them for
us with a Muhammadan protection in our lives and at our deaths and after
our passing and perfect them by our following him, blessings of Allah be
upon him, in words, deeds, behaviour and states, seeking Your noble face,
O Most Noble of the noble. Amin.

بِسْمِ اللهِ الرَّحْمَـٰنِ الرَّحِيمِ الْحَمْدُ لِلَّهِ رَبِّ الْعَـٰلَمِينَ الرَّحْمَـٰنِ الرَّحِيمِ

مَلِكِ يَوْمِ الدِّينِ. إِيَّاكَ نَعْبُدُ وَإِيَّاكَ نَسْتَعِينُ. اِهْدِنَا الصِّرَاطَ

الْمُسْتَقِيمَ صِرَاطَ الَّذِينَ أَنْعَمْتَ عَلَيْهِمْ غَيْرِ الْمَغْضُوبِ عَلَيْهِمْ وَلَا

الضَّالِّينَ. ءَامِينَ.

In the name of Allah, All-Merciful, the Most Merciful. Praise be to Allah,
Lord of the worlds, the All-Merciful, the Most Merciful, the King of
the Day of Judgment. You alone we worship, You alone we ask for help.
Guide us on the Straight Path, the Path of those whom You have blessed,
not of those with anger upon them, nor of the misguided. Amin.

سُبْحَانَ رَبِّكَ رَبِّ الْعِزَّةِ عَمَّا يَصِفُونَ. وَسَلَامٌ عَلَى الْمُرْسَلِينَ.

وَالْحَمْدُ لِلَّهِ رَبِّ الْعَـٰلَمِينَ ○

Glory be to your Lord, the Lord of might, above all else that they
describe. And peace be upon the Messengers.
And praise belongs to Allah, the Lord of all the worlds.

ثُمَّ

Then say:

اَللّٰهُ لَاۤ إِلٰهَ إِلَّا هُوَ. الْحَيُّ الْقَيُّومُ. لَا تَأْخُذُهُۥ سِنَةٌ وَلَا نَوْمٌ. لَّهُۥ مَا فِى السَّمٰوٰتِ وَمَا فِى الْاَرْضِ. مَن ذَا الَّذِى يَشْفَعُ عِندَهُۥۤ إِلَّا بِإِذْنِهِۦ. يَعْلَمُ مَا بَيْنَ أَيْدِيهِمْ وَمَا خَلْفَهُمْ. وَلَا يُحِيطُونَ بِشَىْءٍ مِّنْ عِلْمِهِۦۤ إِلَّا بِمَا شَآءَ. وَسِعَ كُرْسِيُّهُ السَّمٰوٰتِ وَالْاَرْضَ. وَلَا يَئُودُهُۥ حِفْظُهُمَا. وَهُوَ الْعَلِيُّ الْعَظِيمُ.

Allah! There is no god but Him. The Living, the Self-Sustaining. He is not subject to drowsiness or sleep. Everything in the heavens and the earth belongs to Him. Who can intercede with Him except by His permission? He knows what is before them and what is behind them. But they cannot grasp any of His knowledge save what He wills. His Footstool encompasses the heavens and the earth and their preservation does not tire Him. He is the Most High, the Magnificent.

ثُمَّ

Then say:

ءَامَنَ الرَّسُولُ بِمَآ أُنزِلَ إِلَيْهِ مِن رَّبِّهِۦ وَالْمُؤْمِنُونَ. كُلٌّ ءَامَنَ بِاللّٰهِ وَمَلَٰٓئِكَتِهِۦ وَكُتُبِهِۦ وَرُسُلِهِۦ. لَا نُفَرِّقُ بَيْنَ أَحَدٍ مِّن رُّسُلِهِۦ. وَقَالُوا۟ سَمِعْنَا وَأَطَعْنَا. غُفْرَانَكَ رَبَّنَا. وَإِلَيْكَ الْمَصِيرُ.

The Messenger has Iman in what has been sent down to him from his

Lord, and so do the muminun. Each one has Iman in Allah and His angels, and His books and His messengers. We do not differentiate between any of His messengers. They say, 'We hear and we obey. Forgive us, our Lord! You are our journey's end.'

لَا يُكَلِّفُ اللّٰهُ نَفْسًا إِلَّا وُسْعَهَا. لَهَا مَا كَسَبَتْ. وَعَلَيْهَا مَا اكْتَسَبَتْ. رَبَّنَا لَا تُؤَاخِذْنَا إِن نَسِينَا أَوْ أَخْطَأْنَا. رَبَّنَا وَلَا تَحْمِلْ عَلَيْنَا إِصْرًا كَمَا حَمَلْتَهُ عَلَى الَّذِينَ مِن قَبْلِنَا. رَبَّنَا وَلَا تُحَمِّلْنَا مَا لَا طَاقَةَ لَنَا بِهِ. وَاعْفُ عَنَّا. وَاغْفِرْ لَنَا. وَارْحَمْنَا. أَنتَ مَوْلَانَا فَانصُرْنَا عَلَى الْقَوْمِ الْكَافِرِينَ.

Allah does not impose on any self more than it can stand. For it is what it has earned; against it what it has merited. Our Lord, take us not to task if we forget or make a mistake! Our Lord, do not place on us a load like the one You placed on those before us! Our Lord, do not place on us a load we have not the strength to bear! And pardon us; and forgive us; and have mercy on us. You are our Master, so Help us against the people of the kafirun.

ثُمَّ

Then say:

شَهِدَ اللّٰهُ أَنَّهُ لَا إِلَٰهَ إِلَّا هُوَ وَالْمَلَائِكَةُ وَأُولُوا الْعِلْمِ قَائِمًا بِالْقِسْطِ. لَا إِلَٰهَ إِلَّا هُوَ. الْعَزِيزُ الْحَكِيمُ. إِنَّ الدِّينَ عِندَ اللّٰهِ الْإِسْلَامُ.

Allah bears witness that there is no god but Him, as do the angels and the people of knowledge, upholding justice. There is no god but Him, the Almighty, the All-Wise. The Deen with Allah is Islam.

ثُمَّ

Then say:

قُلِ اللَّهُمَّ مَٰلِكَ الْمُلْكِ تُؤْتِي الْمُلْكَ مَن تَشَآءُ وَتَنزِعُ الْمُلْكَ مِمَّن تَشَآءُ وَتُعِزُّ مَن تَشَآءُ وَتُذِلُّ مَن تَشَآءُ بِيَدِكَ الْخَيْرُ. إِنَّكَ عَلَىٰ كُلِّ شَىْءٍ قَدِيرٌ.

Say: 'O Allah! Master of the kingdom! You give sovereignty to whomever You will. You take sovereignty from whomever You will. You exalt whomever You will. You abase whomever You will. All good is in Your hands. You have power over all things.

تُولِجُ الَّيْلَ فِي النَّهَارِ وَتُولِجُ النَّهَارَ فِي الَّيْلِ وَتُخْرِجُ الْحَيَّ مِنَ الْمَيِّتِ وَتُخْرِجُ الْمَيِّتَ مِنَ الْحَيِّ وَتَرْزُقُ مَن تَشَآءُ بِغَيْرِ حِسَابٍ.

You merge the night into the day. You merge the day into the night. You bring out the living from the dead. You bring out the dead from the living. You provide for whomever You will without any reckoning.

لَقَدْ جَآءَكُمْ رَسُولٌ مِّنْ أَنفُسِكُمْ عَزِيزٌ عَلَيْهِ مَا عَنِتُّمْ. حَرِيصٌ عَلَيْكُم. بِالْمُؤْمِنِينَ رَءُوفٌ رَّحِيمٌ.

A Messenger has come to you from among yourselves. Your suffering is
distressing to him; he is deeply concerned for you;
he is gentle and merciful to the muminun.

فَإِن تَوَلَّوْاْ فَقُلْ حَسْبِيَ اللّٰهُ. لَآ إِلٰهَ إِلَّا هُوَ. عَلَيْهِ تَوَكَّلْتُ.
وَهُوَ رَبُّ الْعَرْشِ الْعَظِيمِ.

But if they turn away, say, 'Allah is enough for me. There is no god but
Him. I have put my trust in Him. He is the Lord of the Mighty Throne.'

بِسْمِ اللّٰهِ الرَّحْمٰنِ الرَّحِيمِ قُلْ هُوَ اللّٰهُ أَحَدٌ. اللّٰهُ الصَّمَدُ.
لَمْ يَلِدْ وَلَمْ يُولَدْ. وَلَمْ يَكُن لَّهُ كُفُوًا أَحَدٌ.

In the name of Allah, All-Merciful, Most Merciful, Say: 'He is Allah,
Absolute Oneness. Allah, the Everlasting Sustainer of all. He has not
given birth and was not born. And no one is comparable to Him.'

بِسْمِ اللّٰهِ الرَّحْمٰنِ الرَّحِيمِ قُلْ أَعُوذُ بِرَبِّ الْفَلَقِ مِن شَرِّ مَا خَلَقَ
وَمِن شَرِّ غَاسِقٍ إِذَا وَقَبَ وَمِن شَرِّ النَّفَّاثَاتِ فِى الْعُقَدِ وَمِن شَرِّ
حَاسِدٍ إِذَا حَسَدَ.

In the name of Allah, All-Merciful, Most Merciful, Say: 'I seek refuge
with the Lord of Daybreak, from the evil of what He has created and
from the evil of darkness when it gathers and from the evil of women
who blow on knots and from the evil of an envier when he envies.'

بِسْمِ اللّٰهِ الرَّحْمٰنِ الرَّحِيمِ قُلْ أَعُوذُ بِرَبِّ النَّاسِ مَلِكِ النَّاسِ إِلٰهِ

النَّاسِ مِنْ شَرِّ الْوَسْوَاسِ الْخَنَّاسِ الَّذِي يُوَسْوِسُ فِى صُدُورِ النَّاسِ
مِنَ الْجِنَّةِ وَالنَّاسِ.

In the name of Allah, All-Merciful, Most Merciful, Say: 'I seek refuge
with the Lord of mankind, the King of mankind, the God of mankind,
from the evil of the insidious whisperer who whispers in people's
breasts and comes from the jinn and from mankind.'

اللَّهُمَّ أَنْتَ رَبِّي لَا إِلَهَ إِلَّا أَنْتَ. خَلَقْتَنِي وَأَنَا عَبْدُكَ وَأَنَا عَلَى
عَهْدِكَ وَوَعْدِكَ مَا اسْتَطَعْتُ. أَعُوذُ بِكَ مِنْ شَرِّ مَا صَنَعْتُ. أَبُوءُ
لَكَ بِنِعْمَتِكَ عَلَيَّ وَأَبُوءُ بِذَنْبِي فَاغْفِرْ لِي
فَإِنَّهُ لَا يَغْفِرُ الذُّنُوبَ إِلَّا أَنْتَ.

O Allah, You are my Lord. There is no god but You. You created me and
I am Your slave and I act according to Your covenant and Your promise as
far as I am able. I take refuge with You from the evil of what I have done.
I acknowledge to You Your blessings to me and I acknowledge my wrong
action, so forgive me. None forgives wrong action but You.

رَبِّ اغْفِرْ لِي وَارْحَمْنِي وَتُبْ عَلَيَّ. إِنَّكَ أَنْتَ التَّوَّابُ الرَّحِيمُ.

O my Lord, forgive me and have mercy on me and turn towards me.
You are the One Who Turns, the Compassionate.

بِسْمِ اللهِ الرَّحْمَنِ الرَّحِيمِ الْحَمْدُ لِلّهِ رَبِّ الْعَالَمِينَ الرَّحْمَنِ الرَّحِيمِ
مَلِكِ يَوْمِ الدِّينِ. إِيَّاكَ نَعْبُدُ وَإِيَّاكَ نَسْتَعِينُ. اهْدِنَا الصِّرَاطَ

الْمُسْتَقِيمَ صِرَاطَ الَّذِينَ أَنْعَمْتَ عَلَيْهِمْ غَيْرِ الْمَغْضُوبِ عَلَيْهِمْ وَلَا الضَّالِّينَ. ءَامِين.

In the name of Allah, All-Merciful, the Most Merciful. Praise be to Allah,
Lord of the worlds, the All-Merciful, the Most Merciful, the King of
the Day of Judgment. You alone we worship, You alone we ask for help.
Guide us on the Straight Path, the Path of those whom You have blessed,
not of those with anger upon them, nor of the misguided. Amin.

سُبْحَانَ رَبِّكَ رَبِّ الْعِزَّةِ عَمَّا يَصِفُونَ. وَسَلَامٌ عَلَى الْمُرْسَلِينَ.
وَالْحَمْدُ لِلَّهِ رَبِّ الْعَلَمِينَ.

Glory be to your Lord, the Lord of might, above all else that they
describe. And peace be upon the Messengers.
And praise belongs to Allah, the Lord of all the worlds.

بِسْمِ اللهِ الرَّحْمَنِ الرَّحِيمِ الْحَمْدُ لِلَّهِ الَّذِي خَلَقَ السَّمَوَاتِ
وَالْأَرْضَ وَجَعَلَ الظُّلُمَاتِ وَالنُّورَ
ثُمَّ الَّذِينَ كَفَرُوا بِرَبِّهِمْ يَعْدِلُونَ.

In the name of Allah, All-Merciful, Most Merciful,
praise belongs to Allah, Who created the heavens and the earth
and appointed the shadows and the light,
then the ones who cover over ascribe equals to their Lord.

هُوَ الَّذِي خَلَقَكُمْ مِنْ طِينٍ ثُمَّ قَضَى أَجَلًا.

وَأَجَلٌ مُسَمًّى عِنْدَهُ، ثُمَّ أَنْتُمْ تَمْتَرُونَ.

It is He Who created you from clay, then determined a term. And a term is stated with Him. Yet thereafter you doubt.

وَهُوَ اللهُ، فِى السَّمَوَاتِ وَفِى الأَرْضِ يَعْلَمُ سِرَّكُمْ وَجَهْرَكُمْ وَيَعْلَمُ مَا تَكْسِبُونَ.

He is Allah. In the heavens and in the earth He knows your secrets and what you publish and He knows what you are earning.

اَلْحَمْدُ لِلَّهِ الَّذِي هَدَانَا لِهَذَا وَمَا كُنَّا لِنَهْتَدِيَ لَوْلَاۤ أَنْ هَدَانَا اللهُ. لَقَدْ جَاءَتْ رُسُلُ رَبِّنَا بِالْحَقِّ. (ثلاثا)

Praise belongs to Allah Who guided us to this, and had Allah not guided us we would surely never have been guided. Indeed our Lord's messengers came with the truth.

وَبَعْدَ كُلِّ مَرَّةٍ تَقُولُ

Then each time say:

اَللَّهُمَّ لَكَ الْحَمْدُ. (ثلاثا)

O Allah, praise belongs to You. (3)

ثُمَّ تَقُولُ

Then say:

اَللَّهُمَّ مَآ أَنْعَمْتَ بِهِ فَنْكَ بِكَ لَكَ وَحْدَكَ لَا شَرِيكَ لَكَ.

لَآ أُحْصِي ثَنَآءً عَلَيْكَ. أَنْتَ كَمَآ أَثْنَيْتَ عَلَىٰ نَفْسِكَ.

O Allah, what You have bestowed on us of blessing is from You, by You
and Yours alone. There is no partner with You. I am unable to praise
You properly; You are as You praise Yourself. (3)

مَا شَآءَ اللهُ. لَا قُوَّةَ إِلَّا بِاللهِ. (ثلاثا) الْحَمْدُ لِلَّهِ رَبِّ العَالَمِينَ.

It is as Allah wills. There is no strength but with Allah. (3)
Praise belongs to Allah, the Lord of the worlds.

ثُمَّ تَرْفَعُ يَدَيْكَ مُصَلِّيًا عَلَى النَّبِيّ صَلَّى اللهُ عَلَيْهِ وَسَلَّمَ دَاعِيًا لِآلِ البَيْتِ
وَلِآلِ جَانِبِ اللهِ وَالمَشَائِخِ وَالوَالِدَيْنِ وَالإِخْوَانِ وَالأَحْبَابِ وَلِكَافَّةِ المُسْلِمِينَ
وَالمُسْلِمَاتِ: تَقُولُ

*Then raise your hands and pray for the Prophet ﷺ and for the people of the house
and for the near-to-Allah and the Shaykhs, parents, brothers and loved ones, and
all the muslims, men and women. Then say:*

اللَّهُمَّ صَلِّ عَلَىٰ سَيِّدِنَا مُحَمَّدٍ عَبْدِكَ وَرَسُولِكَ النَّبِيّ الأُمِّيّ
وَعَلَىٰ ءَالِهِ وَصَحْبِهِ وَسَلِّمْ. (ثلاثا)

O Allah, bless our master Muhammad, Your slave and Your Messenger,
the unlettered Prophet, and his family and Companions,
and grant them peace. (3)

وَتَزِيدُ بَعْدَ الثَّالِثَةِ: تَسْلِيمًا ثُمَّ تَقُولُ:

Add "tasleema" after the third, and then say:

اَللّٰهُمَّ إِنَّا نَسْأَلُكَ إِيمَانًا دَائِمًا. وَنَسْأَلُكَ قَلْبًا خَاشِعًا. وَنَسْأَلُكَ عِلْمًا
نَافِعًا. وَنَسْأَلُكَ يَقِينًا صَادِقًا. وَنَسْأَلُكَ دِينًا قَيِّمًا. وَنَسْأَلُكَ الْعَافِيَةَ
مِنْ كُلِّ بَلِيَّةٍ. وَنَسْأَلُكَ تَمَامَ الْعَافِيَةِ. وَنَسْأَلُكَ دَوَامَ الْعَافِيَةِ.
وَنَسْأَلُكَ الشُّكْرَ عَلَى الْعَافِيَةِ.
وَنَسْأَلُكَ الْغِنٰى عَنِ النَّاسِ.

Allah, we ask You for a constant Iman. We ask you for a humble heart.
We ask You for useful knowledge. We ask You for genuine certainty.
We ask You for correct Deen. We ask You for a safe outcome from
every trial. We ask You for complete wellbeing. We ask You for
enduring wellbeing. We ask You for gratitude for wellbeing. We ask
You for freedom from need of people.

اَللّٰهُمَّ أَحْسِنْ عَاقِبَتَنَا فِي الْأُمُورِ كُلِّهَا
وَأَجِرْنَا مِنْ خِزْيِ الدُّنْيَا وَعَذَابِ الْآخِرَةِ.

Allah, make good the outcome of all our affairs,
and protect us from the shame of the world,
and from punishment in the world to come.

اَللَّهُمَّ يَا لَطِيفُ نَسْأَلُكَ اللُّطْفَ

فِي مَا جَرَتْ بِهِ المَقَادِيرُ. (ثَلَاثًا)

Allah, O Latif, we ask You for lutf in what the decrees entail. (3)

سُبْحَانَ رَبِّكَ رَبِّ الْعِزَّةِ عَمَّا يَصِفُونَ. وَسَلَامٌ عَلَى الْمُرْسَلِينَ.

وَالْحَمْدُ لِلَّهِ رَبِّ الْعَالَمِينَ ۝

Glory be to your Lord, the Lord of might, above all else that they
describe. And peace be upon the Messengers.

And praise belongs to Allah, the Lord of all the worlds.

The Wird of Fajr
أذكار الفجر

وَيَنْبَغِي لِكُلِّ فَقِيرٍ أَنْ لَا يَتْرُكَ حَظَّهُ مِنْ رُكَيْعَاتٍ قُبَيْلَ الْفَجْرِ، ثُمَّ يُصَلِّي عَلَى
النَّبِيّ صَلَّى اللهُ عَلَيْهِ وَسَلَّمَ بِالصَّلَاةِ الْمَشِيشِيَّةِ الْمَشْهُورَةِ ثُمَّ يَذْكُرُ مِنَ الِاسْمِ
الْمُفْرَدِ سِتَّمِائَةً وَسِتِّينَ مَرَّةً

No faqeer should leave out his portion of rak'ats shortly before Fajr, then he
should ask for blessings on the Prophet ﷺ with the well known
Salat al-Mashishiyya. Then he should invoke the Singular Name
six hundred and sixty times.

ثُمَّ تَقُولُ بَعْدَ رَغِيبَةِ الْفَجْرِ

Then you say after the two sunna rak'ats of Fajr:

يَا حَيُّ يَا قَيُّومُ لَا إِلَهَ إِلَّا أَنْتَ. (إِحْدَى وَأَرْبَعِينَ مَرَّةً)

O Living, O Self-subsistent! There is no god but You. (41)

ثُمَّ تَقُولُ

Then say:

سُبْحَانَ اللهِ وَبِحَمْدِهِ سُبْحَانَ اللهِ الْعَظِيمِ. أَسْتَغْفِرُ اللهَ. (عشرا)

Glory be to Allah by His praise, Glory be to Allah the Vast. I seek
forgiveness of Allah. (10)

ثُمَّ تَقُولُ

Then say:

اللهُ (سبعا)

Allah (7)

وَتَعْقِبُهُ بِالتَّهْلِيلِ وَالْابْتِهَالِ حَتَّى تُقَامَ صَلَاةُ الْفَرِيضَةِ.

*Follow that with La ilaha illa' llah and with supplication
until the iqama of the obligatory salat.*

Commentary on the Wird

تَائِيَّةُ الْوِرْدِ الشَّرِيفِ

يَقُولُ عُبَيْدُ اللهِ أَعْنِي مُحَمَّدًا

هُوَ ابْنُ حَبِيبٍ قَاصِدًا لِلنَّصِيحَةِ

The lowly slave of Allah, Muhammad ibn al-Habib,
says intending counsel:

أَيَا صَاحِبِي عِشْ فِي هَنَاءٍ وَنِعْمَةٍ

إِذَا كُنْتَ فِينَا ذَا اعْتِقَادٍ وَنِيَّةٍ

O my companion! Live in joy and serenity
if you are among us as one with firm belief and intention,

وَأَخْلَصْتَ فِي الْوُدِّ الَّذِي هُوَ رُكْنُنَا

فِي سَيْرِ طَرِيقِ اللهِ مِنْ غَيْرِ مِرْيَةِ

And if you are sincere in the love which is, without doubt,
our firm support while travelling on the Tariq of Allah,

وَكُنْتَ قَوِيَّ الْعَزْمِ فِي الْوِرْدِ حَاضِرًا

بِقَلْبٍ لِتَحْقِيقِ الْمَعَانِي الدَّقِيقَةِ

And if you have a strong resolve to recite the Wird, and are
present with an attentive heart to realise its subtle meanings,

وَأَحْضَرْتَ مَعْنَى الذِّكْرِ فِي كُلِّ مَرَّةٍ

تَكُونُ مُعَانًا فِي الْأُمُورِ بِسُرْعَةَ

And if at all times you call to mind the meaning of the dhikr,
you will be quickly helped in your affairs.

فَمِفْتَاحُ وِرْدٍ قُلْ صَلَاةٌ تَعَوُّذٌ

وَبَسْمِلْ وَحَوْقِلْ تُكْفَ كُلَّ بَلِيَّةٍ

The key of the Wird is the prayer on the Prophet, the taking refuge,
the 'Bismillah', the 'no power' – and that is enough for every problem.

فَتَبْدَا بِالِاسْتِغْفَارِ أَوَّلَ وِرْدِنَا

تَحُوزُ بِهِ نَيْلًا لِكُلِّ فَضِيلَةٍ

You begin our Wird with the Istighfar,
and by it you will obtain every good quality.

وَمَعْنَاهُ سِتْرُ اللهِ لِلْعَبْدِ عَنْ ذَنْبٍ

فَيَحْفَظُهُ مِنْ كُلِّ هَوْلٍ وَفِتْنَةَ

Its real meaning is Allah's veil over the wrong action of His slave,
and so it protects him from every terror and trial.

فَلَا هَمَّ يَبْقَى مَعْ دَوَامِكَ ذِكْرَهُ

وَلَا رَيْبَ فِي تَسْهِيلِ رِزْقٍ بِكَثْرَةِ

No care can remain when you persevere in His dhikr,
and no doubt can remain when your needs are amply met.

وَبَعْدَ الْفَرَاغِ مِنْهُ صَلِّ عَلَى النَّبِي

صَلَاةَ مُحِبٍّ رَاسِخٍ فِي الْمَحَبَّةِ

After you finish this, ask for blessing on the Prophet
with the prayer of a lover firmly rooted in love –

وَمَعْنَاهَا رَحْمَةٌ تُنَاسِبُ قَدْرَهُ

وَقَدْرُهُ يَعْلُو قَدْرَ كُلِّ الْخَلِيقَةِ

Its true meaning is the mercy that befits his rank,
and his rank is above the rank of every person.

وَتُشْخِصْهُ فِي مِرْآةِ قَلْبِكَ دَائِمًا

وَعَوِّلْ عَلَيْهِ فِي الْوُصُولِ لِحَضْرَةِ

Constantly see him in the mirror of your heart
and rely on him for attainment of the Presence.

وَهَيْلَلَةٌ بَعْدَ الصَّلَاةِ عَلَى النَّبِي

فَتَنْفِي بِهَا وَهْمًا عَنْ عَيْنِ الْبَصِيرَةِ

After the prayer on the Prophet, recite 'La ilaha illa'llah'.
By it you will expel illusion from the inner eye.

وَتُسْرِعُ فِي نَفْيِ السِّوَىٰ وَهْوَ قَاطِعُ
لِقَوْمٍ طَرِيقِ الْحَقِّ مِنْ غَيْرِ مِرْيَةِ

And you will be swift to negate otherness for there is no doubt
that it is a screen to the people on the Tariq al-Haqq.

وَتَشْهَدُ رَبًّا قَدْ تَجَلَّتْ صِفَاتُهُ
بِأَسْرَارِ أَكْوَانٍ وَأَنْوَارِ جَنَّةِ

And you will witness a Lord Whose Attributes have been manifested
by the secrets of phenomena and the lights of the Garden.

وَتُدْرِكُ سِرًّا لَيْسَ يَعْرِفُ قَدْرَهُ
سِوَىٰ عَارِفٍ بِاللهِ صَاحِبِ نَظْرَةِ

And you will grasp a secret whose true value is only known
by an 'arif bi'llah who possesses vision.

وَسَبِّحْ بِتَسْبِيحِ الالَهِ فِي كُتْبِهِ
وَإِيَّاكَ تَنْزِيهًا بِعَقْلٍ وَفِكْرَةِ

Glorify Him with Allah's glorification that is in His Book,
but take care not to perform tanzih with reason and thinking.

وَنَزِّهْ بِمَا قَدْ نَزَّهَ الْحَقُّ نَفْسَهُ
وَفَوِّضْ وَنَزِّهْ عَنْ حُدُوثٍ وَشِرْكَةِ

And do it in the way that the Haqq has purified Himself –
entrust yourself to Him, and free Him from being-in-time and shirk.

وَكُنْ حَامِدًا مُسْتَحْضِرَ الْعَجْزِ فِي الثَّنَا

كَمَا جَاءَ وَارِدًا عَنْ خَيْرِ الْخَلِيقَة

Give praise while you bear in mind your inability to praise
as it was reported by the Best of Creation.

وَحَسْبَلَةٌ بَعْدَ الْفَرَاغِ مِنَ الْوِرْدِ

فَتَذْكُرُ مِنْهَا عَدَّ سَجِّي بَنِيَّة

After finishing the Wird say 'Hasbuna'llah'
and say it with firm intention seventy-three times.

وَقَدْ وَعَدَ الْحَقُّ الْجَلِيلُ كِفَايَةً

لِذَاكِرِهَا مِنْ غَيْرِ قَيْدٍ بِحَالَة

The Majestic Truth has promised the dhakir who recites it
that he will have what he needs, not limited to any state.

فَقَدْ طَفَأَتْ نَارُ الْخَلِيلِ بِسِرِّهَا

وَنَالَ الْحَبِيبُ مِنْهَا كُلَّ فَضِيلَة

It extinguished the fire of the Khalil (Ibrahim) by its secret,
and from it the Habib (Muhammad) was given every gift.

فَفِي وَقْتِنَا هَذَا يُرَجَّحُ ذِكْرُهَا

عَلَى الذِّكْرِ بِالْأَحْزَابِ أَوْ بِوَظِيفَة

In this time of ours, its dhikr and invocation
take preference over Hizbs or Wazifas.

وَإِنْ شِئْتَ إِسْرَاعًا لِفَهْمِ الْحَقِيقَةِ

فَوَاظِبْ عَلَى الِاسْمِ الْعَظِيمِ بِهِمَّةِ

If you wish to hasten understanding of the Haqiqa,
then with Himma persevere in repeating the Tremendous Name.

وَشَخِّصْ حُرُوفَ الِاسْمِ فِي الْقَلْبِ دَائِمًا

وَرَاجِعْهُ فِي النِّسْيَانِ فِي كُلِّ مَرَّةِ

Always mirror the letters of the Name in your heart,
and bring it back every time you forget.

وَلَا تَلْتَفِتْ لِلْغَيْرِ إِنَّهُ قَاطِعٌ

وَلَوْ كَانَ مَحْمُودًا فَأَحْرَىٰ لِظُلْمَةِ

Do not turn to otherness – it is indeed a barrier.
Even when praiseworthy, it is still more suited to darkness.

فَذِكْرُهُ عِنْدَ الْقَوْمِ يُغْنِي عَنْ غَيْرِهِ

وَلَا عَكْسَ عِ إِنْ كُنْتَ صَاحِبَ هِمَّةِ

To the People, His dhikr frees from what is other-than-Him,
and there is no opposite to Allah; pay attention if you possess himma.

وَرَاقِبْهُ عِنْدَ الذِّكْرِ وَافْنَ عَنْ غَيْرِهِ

وَلَا غَيْرَ إِلَّا مِنْ تَوَهُّمِ كَثْرَةِ

Watch for Him in the dhikr and be annihilated to other-than-Him,
and there is no other except for the illusion of multiplicity.

وَمَا هِيَ إِلَّا وَحْدَةٌ قَدْ تَكَثَّرَتْ

بِمُقْتَضَىٰ أَسْمَاءٍ وَءَاثَارِ قُدْرَةِ

Multiplicity is only oneness multiplied in accordance
with the Names and the traces of Divine Power.

وَمَظْهَرُهَا الاَعْلَى الرَّسُولُ مُحَمَّدٌ

عَلَيْهِ صَلَاةُ اللهِ فِي كُلِّ لَحْظَةِ

Its highest place of manifestation is the Messenger Muhammad,
may the blessings of Allah be upon him at every instant,

وَءَالِهِ وَالاَصْحَابِ مَا حَنَّ ذَاكِرٌ

لِذِكْرِ إِلَهِ الْعَرْشِ فِي كُلِّ حَالَةِ

and on his family and Companions as long as there is a dhakir
who yearns to do the dhikr of the God of the Throne in every state.

طَرِيقَتُنَا تَعْلُو الطَّرَائِقَ كُلَّهَا

لَتَحْرِيرِنَا الْمَقْصُودَ أَوَّلَ مَرَّةِ

Our Tariqa greatly surpasses all other paths –
because we obtain the goal we desire, first time.

وَلِلْجَمعِ بَيْنَ الْمَشْهِدَينِ بِلَا رَيْبِ

فَمَشْهَدُ حَقٍّ ثُمَّ مَشْهَدُ شِرْعَةِ

And it unites the two aspects without any doubt –
the aspect of the Haqiqa and the aspect of the Shari'a.

وَأَسْأَلُ رَبِّ اللهَ فَتْحًا إِلَهِيًّا

لِكُلِّ مُرِيدٍ صَادِقٍ فِي الطَّرِيقَةِ

I ask Allah, my Lord, to grant a Divine opening
to each and every sincere murid on the Tariqa,

وَأَنْ يُرْشِدَ الاِخْوَانَ لِلْجَمْعِ دَائِمًا

عَلَى كُلِّ مَا يُرْضِي إِلَهَ الْبَرِيَّةِ

And that He always guide the brotherhood to stay together,
holding to what is pleasing to the God of creation.

وَأُهْدِي سَلاَمِي لِلَّذِينَ تَعَلَّقُوا

بِأَذْكَارِ خَيْرِ الْخَلْقِ مِنْ كُلِّ فِرْقَةِ

I convey my greetings of peace to those of every group
devoted to the dhikrs of the Best of Creation.

فَتَابِعْهُ إِنْ كُنْتَ الْمُحِبَّ لِرَبِّنَا

يُثِبْكَ عَلَى ذَاكَ الاِلَهُ بِنَظْرَةِ

Follow him if you are a lover of our Lord,
and Allah will reward you with a glance from Him.

فَقَدْ كَمُلَتْ مُسْتَغْفِرًا مِنْ توهُّمٍ

لِغَيْرِ وُجُودِ الْحَقِّ فِي كُلِّ لَمْحَةِ ۞

The song is complete and I seek forgiveness for any illusion
of other than the existence of the Haqq in every glance.

The Greater Qasida

وله رضي الله عنه القصيدة المسماة
بالتائية الكبرى

فَإِنْ شِئْتَ أَنْ تَرْقَىٰ رُقِيَّ الأَحِبَّةِ
فَعَرِّجْ عَلَىٰ لَيْلَىٰ بِصِدْقِ الْمَوَدَّةِ

If you wish to ascend as the lovers ascend,
turn to Layla with complete sincerity in love.

وَكُلَّ عَذُولٍ فِي مَحَبَّتِهَا انْبُذَنْ
وَسَافِرْ إِلَى الأَحْبَابِ فِي كُلِّ بَلْدَةِ

Dismiss all who criticise Her love,
and travel to the lovers in every land.

وَلَوْ أَنَّ صِدْقَ الْحُبِّ فِيكَ حَقِيقَةً
رَأَيْتَ بِهَا الأَحْبَابَ مِنْ غَيْرِ رِحْلَةِ

If your sincerity in love were real, by it
you would see the lovers without journeying.

وَلَوْ أَنَّ عَيْنَ الْقَلْبِ مِنْكَ تَطَهَّرَتْ
لَأَبْصَرَتِ الأَنْوَارَ مِنْهَا تَجَلَّتْ

If your heart's eye had been purified
you would see the lights manifested from Her.

فَكُنْ عَبْدَهَا شُكْرًا بِلَا رُؤْيَةِ السِّوَا
وَمَا بِكَ مِنْ نُعْمَىٰ فَمِنْهَا تَبَدَّتْ

Be Her slave gratefully without seeing otherness.
Every aspect of your happiness has come from Her.

وَإِيَّاكَ تَلْبِيسَ الْخَوَاطِرِ إِنَّهَا
تَمُوهُ نُصْحًا وَهْوَ أَعْظَمُ فِرْيَةِ

Beware of the deceptions of thoughts which arise.
They weaken good counsel and they are the greatest lies.

نُخَالِلْ أَخَا صِدْقٍ يُمَيِّزُ بَيْنَهَا
وَيُذْهِبُ عَنْكَ مَا أَتَاكَ بِشُبْهَةِ

Take a sincere brother as your intimate who can distinguish
between them and dispel any doubts you have.

وَهَيْلَلَةٌ تَنْفِي جَمِيعَ الْوَسَاوِسِ
بِتَلْقِينِ شَيْخٍ عَارِفٍ بِالْحَقِيقَةِ

'La ilaha illa'llah' banishes all whisperings
with the instruction of a Shaykh who knows the Haqiqa.

وَءَايَاتُهُ نُورٌ يَلُوحُ بِظَاهِرٍ

وَسِرٌّ بَدَا مِنْ بَاطِنٍ مَعَ هِمَّةٍ

His signs are a light which shines, appearing outwardly
and a secret which appears inwardly with himma.

وَتَرْقِيَةٌ بِاللَّحْظِ قَبْلَ تَلَفُّظٍ

فَإِنْ كَانَ مِنْهُ اللَّفْظُ جَآءَ بِحُلَّةٍ

He elevates you with a glance even before he speaks,
and if he speaks it brings a Robe of Honour.

وَأَعْنِي بِهَا الْأَنْوَارَ تَسْرِي بِسُرْعَةٍ

لِقَلْبِ مُرِيدِ الْحَقِّ مِنْ غَيْرِ شِرْكَةٍ

By that I mean the lights which flow rapidly
into the heart of the murid seeking the truth without shirk.

وَزُهْدُهُ فِي الْأَكْوَانِ عُمْدَةُ سَيْرِهِ

وَشُغْلٌ بِإِفْرَادِ الْحَبِيبِ بِرُؤْيَةٍ

His zuhd among people is the staff of his journey
and his occupation with seeking the Beloved alone in vision.

وَتَصْرِيحُهُ بِالْإِذْنِ مِنْ خَيْرِ أُمَّةٍ

عَلَيْهِ اعْتِمَادُ الصَّادِقِينَ الْأَجِلَّةِ

His speech is by Idhn from the Best of the Umma
upon whom the glorious truthful ones depend.

فَإِنْ حَصَلَ الْمَقْصُودُ مِمَّا ذَكَرْتَهُ

فَبَادِرْ وَأَعْطِ النَّفْسَ مِنْ غَيْرِ مُهْلَةِ

If you attain the goal of finding someone like this,
then set out and offer up the self without delay.

وَلَا تَعْتَبِرْ شَيْئًا سِوَىٰ مَا رَسَمْتَهُ

فَفِيهِ الَّذِي يُغْنِي وَكُلُّ الْمَسَرَّةِ

Consider nothing except what I have described here,
for it is enough, and it contains every happiness.

فَإِنْ لَمْ تَجِدْ مِمَّا ذَكَرْتُ فَإِنَّنِي

سَأَشْرَحُ نَهْجَ الْحَقِّ مِنْ غَيْرِ مِرْيَةِ

If you have not found such a man,
then let me describe to you the certain path of truth.

فَأَوَّلُ فِعْلِ الْمَرْءِ فِي بَدْءِ سَيْرِهِ

مُجَانَبَةُ الْأَشْرَارِ مِنْ كُلِّ فِرْقَةِ

At the beginning of his journey a man's first act
is to avoid the evil people of every group.

وَشُغْلٌ بِذِكْرِ اللهِ جَلَّ جَلَالُهُ

فَفِيهِ الدَّوَا مِنْ كُلِّ عَيْبٍ وَعِلَّةِ

He should busy himself with dhikr of Allah, may He be glorified,
for in that lies the remedy for every fault and ill.

وَخِدْمَةُ خَيْرِ الْخَلْقِ أَعْظَمُ قُرْبَةٍ

فَفِيهِ مِنَ الْخَيْرَاتِ أَعْلَا مَزِيَّةٍ

The greatest offering is to serve the Best of Creation.
Therein lies the highest excellence in good deeds.

فَشَاهِدْهُ فِي الْاَكْوَانِ قَدْ عَمَّ نُورُهُ

وَمِنْهُ أَتَى الْإِمْدَادُ فِي كُلِّ لَحْظَةٍ

Witness him in created forms where his light has spread.
Help is coming from him in every instant.

وَحَكِّمْهُ فِي التَّشْرِيعِ دُونَ تَكَاسُلٍ

وَجَانِبْ مُرَادَ النَّفْسِ أَصْلَ الْبَلِيَّةِ

Make him the arbiter in following the Shari'a without laziness,
and avoid the will of the self, the source of grief.

وَغَلِّبْ جَنَابَ الْحَقِّ عِنْدَ نِزَاعِهَا

وَلَا تَغْتَرِرْ بِالْعِلْمِ إِلَّا بِخَشْيَةٍ

Let the truth take over in the struggle with the self.
Do not be deceived by knowledge without fear of Allah.

وَأَعْظَمُ ذَنْبِ الْعَبْدِ رُؤْيَةُ نَفْسِهِ

فَفِيهَا مِنَ الْاَخْبَاثِ كُلُّ شَنِيعَةٍ

The worst thing the slave can do is look at his self.
It contains every dreadful and atrocious thing!

وَوَحْدَةُ فِعْلِ اللهِ تَنْفِي رُسُومَهَا

وَتَطْوِي جَمِيعَ الْكَوْنِ عَنْهَا فِي لَحْظَةِ

In one instant the unity of the Act of Allah
wipes out every trace of the self and engulfs all creation.

فَعَوِّلْ عَلَى التَّوْحِيدِ وَاتْرُكْ شُكُوكَهَا

تَفُزْ بِالَّذِي قَدْ فَازَ كُلُّ الاَجِلَّةِ

Rely on Tawhid and leave behind the doubts of the self
and you will achieve what all the noble ones have achieved.

فَإِنْ تَصْدُرِ الاَعْمَالُ مِنْهُمْ كَآلَةٍ

تُحَرِّكُهَا الاَقْدَارُ مِنْ غَيْرِ رِيبَةِ

When they make any action there is no question
but that they are just like instruments moved by Divine decrees,

فَتَوْبَتُهُمْ لِلَّهِ بِاللهِ مُطْلَقًا

وَخَوْفُهُمْ تَعْظِيمُ عِزٍّ وَهِيبَةِ

And their tawba is to Allah by Allah absolutely.
Their khawf is in feeling His immense might and awesomeness.

رَجَاؤُهُمْ حُسْنُ الْيَقِينِ بِوَعْدِهِ

وَشِدَّةُ إِتْعَابِ الْجُسُومِ فِي خِدْمَةِ

Their raja' is complete certainty in His promise
and the hardship and fatigue of their bodies in His service.

وَشُكْرُهُمْ شُغْلٌ بِرُؤْيَةِ مُنْعِمٍ

وَغِيبَتُهُمْ عَنْ كُلِّ ضِيقٍ وَنِعْمَةِ

Their shukr is in being occupied in seeing the Bestower of blessings,
and in being detached from both constriction and blessing.

وَصَبْرُهُمْ حُسْنُ الرِّضَى بِمَقَادِرٍ

وَلَيْسَ لَهُمْ تَدْبِيرُ سُقْمٍ وَصِحَّةِ

Their sabr is complete contentment with events.
They seek no control over either sickness or good health.

تَوَكُّلُهُمْ تَفْوِيضُ كُلِّ أُمُورِهِمْ

لِمَنْ هُوَ أَدْرَى بِالْأُمُورِ الْخَفِيَّةِ

Their tawakkul consists in handing over all their affairs
to the One Who has the best knowledge of hidden matters.

وَزُهْدُهُمْ يَأْسٌ مِمَّا لَمْ يَكُنْ لَهُمْ

بِسَابِقِ عِلْمِ اللهِ مِنْ بَرْمِ قِسْمَةِ

Their zuhd is to renounce everything except
what Allah has decreed for them in His fore-knowledge.

مَحَبَّتُهُمْ سُكْرٌ بِحُسْنِ جَمَالِهِ

وَفِيهَا مَقَامُ الْأُنْسِ أَشْرَفُ حِلْيَةِ

Their love is intoxication with the perfection of His beauty.
This love contains the Maqam al-Uns, the noblest adornment.

وَبَسْطٌ وَإِدْلَالٌ وَتَكْلِيمُ حِبِّهِمْ
وَأَسْرَارُهَا تَسْرِي إِلَىٰ غَيْرِ غَايَةِ

And bast, liberation, and speaking with their Beloved
– the secrets of love endlessly flow on and on.

فَنَافِسْهُمْ فِيهَا بِحُسْنِ تَأَدُّبٍ
وَأَحْسِنْ لِأَحْبَابِ الْحَبِيبِ بِفَضْلَةِ

Outdo them in actions with the best adab.
Be generous and treat the lovers of the Beloved well.

فَلَوْ عَرَفَ الْإِنْسَانُ قِيمَةَ قَلْبِهِ
لَأَنْفَقَ كُلَّ الْكُلِّ مِنْ غَيْرِ فَتْرَةِ

For a man would unceasingly spend all he had –
if he only understood the secret of his own heart.

وَلَوْ أَدْرَكَ الانْسَانُ لَذَّةَ سِرِّهِ
لَقَارَنَ أَنْفَاسَ الْخُرُوجِ بِعَبْرَةِ

If a man could but grasp the bliss of his secret
he would shed a tear with every breath he breathed.

وَطَارَ مِنْ الْجِسْمِ الَّذِي صَارَ قَفْصَهُ
بِأَجْنِحَةِ الْأَفْكَارِ مُنْتَهَىٰ سِدْرَةِ

Then, his body become his cage, he would fly from it
with the wings of contemplation to the Furthest Lote-Tree.

66

وَجَالَ نَوَاحِي الْعَرْشِ وَالْكُرْسِيِّ الَّذِي
تَضَاءَلَتِ الاَجْرَامُ عَنْهُ كَحَلْقَةٍ

He would freely roam around the Throne and the Footstool
which make the heavenly bodies appear like a small ring.

وَشَاهَدَ أَفْلَاكًا وَسِرَّ بُرُوجِهَا
وَشِدَّةَ إِفْرَاطِ الْمُرُورِ بِسُرْعَةٍ

He would see the spheres and the secrets of their constellations
and the meaning of their tremendously rapid movement.

وَزَالَ حِجَابُ اللَّوْحِ عَنْ طَيِّ سِرِّهِ
فَفَاحَتْ عُلُومُ الْكَشْفِ مِنْ غَيْرِ سُتْرَةٍ

The veil of the Tablet of Forms would be lifted from his secret
and so the hidden knowledges would emerge uncovered.

فَلَوْ كَانَتِ الاَشْجَارُ أَقْلَامَ كَتْبِهَا
وَمِدَادُهَا الْبَحْرُ الْمُحِيطُ لَجَفَّتِ

Had the trees been the pens to write it and their ink
the oceans, they would have dried up.

وَزَارَ مِنَ الْمَعْمُورِ أَمْلَاكَهُ الَّتِي
تَنُوفُ عَلَى الاَعْدَادِ مِنْ غَيْرِ غَايَةٍ

And he would visit the Frequented House
with its countless myriad angels.

67

وَوَافَىٰ دُخُولَ حَضْرَةِ الْقُدْسِ طَالِبًا

لِتَطْهِيرِ سِرِّ السِّرِّ مِنْ كُلِّ وَقْفَةِ

And, in his quest to purify the secret of his secret from every way-stage
he finally comes to the door to the pure Presence.

فَهَذَا مَحَطُّ الْقَوْمِ عِنْدَ سَرَائِهِمْ

بِأَرْوَاحِهِمْ مَحَلُّ كَتْمٍ وَحَيْرَةِ

Now, this Station of the People in the journey of their spirits
is the Station of concealment and bewilderment.

وَمِنْ بَعْدِهَا الْعِلْمُ الَّذِي لَا يَبثُّه

سِوَىٰ مَنْ لَهُ الْإِذْنُ الصَّرِيحُ بِرُؤْيَةِ

After it comes knowledge – which may not be divulged
except by the one who in vision has received a clear Idhn.

وَفِي الْأَرْضِ ءَايَاتٌ لِكُلِّ مُفَكِّرٍ

عَجَائِبُهَا تَمْضِي إِلَىٰ أَعْلَا عِبْرَةِ

The earth is full of signs for all who look and reflect.
Its marvels can take one to the highest teaching –

فَأَسْمَاءُ رَبِّ الْعَرْشِ قَدْ عَمَّ نُورُهَا

بِأَجْزَائِهَا مَا بَيْنَ خَافٍ وَشُهْرَةِ

For the light of the Names of the Lord of the Throne
extends throughout all its known and hidden parts.

فَلَوْ جُلْتَ فِي الْمِيَاهِ مَعْ أَصْلِ نَشْئِهَا

وَتَرْبِيَةِ الاشْيَاءِ مِنْهَا بِحِكْمَةِ

If you were to reflect on the oceans and their origin,
and how things were fostered from out of them with wisdom,

حَكَمْتَ بِعَجْزِ الْكُلِّ عَنْ دَرْكِ سِرِّهَا

وَبُحْتَ بِتَخْصِيصِ الالَهِ بِقُدْرَةِ

then you would know that no one is capable of grasping their secret
and you would affirm that power belongs to Allah alone.

وَأَطْلِقْ عِنَانَ الْفِكْرِ عِنْدَ جِبَالِهَا

تَجِدْهَا هِيَ الاوْتَادُ مِنْ غَيْرِ مِرْيَةِ

Let your thoughts flow freely regarding its mountains
and you will find that they are the pegs without doubt.

وَمَا حَوَتِ الازْهَارُ مِنْ حُسْنِ مَنْظَرٍ

وَكَثْرَةِ تَنْوِيعِ الثِّمَارِ الْبَدِيعَةِ

Look at the beauty of the appearance of the flowers,
and the marvellous variety of different fruits.

وَمَا أَظْهَرَتْ مِنْ كُلِّ شَيْءٍ يُرَىٰ بِهَا

وَكُلُّ أَتَىٰ مِنْ عَيْنِ عِزٍّ وَسَطْوَةِ

Look at every visible manifestation!
It all gushes from the fount of energy and power.

فَشَاهِدْ جَمَالَ الْحَقِّ عِنْدَ لَحَاظِهَا

وَإِيَّاكَ تَنْكِيفًا عَلَى أَدْنَى ذَرَّةٍ

Consider all this and then see the beauty of the truth.
Take care – you cannot despise even the lowest atom.

فَمَا قَامَتِ الأَشْيَاءُ إِلَّا بِرَبِّهَا

فَيَا حَيُّ يَا قَيُّومُ أَبْلَغُ حُجَّةٍ

Things have no existence except through their Lord.
O Living! O Eternal! Your own most eloquent proof!

فَفِي النَّفْسِ ءَايَاتٌ لِكُلِّ مُفَكِّرٍ

فَفِيهَا انْطَوَى الْكَوْنُ الْكَبِيرُ بِرُمَّةٍ

There are signs in the self for any who ponders it
because the entire universe is contained in it.

وَزَادَتْ بِوُسْعِ الْحَقِّ عِنْدَ تَطَهُّرٍ

وَذَا قُلْ بِلَا كَيْفٍ وَأَيْنٍ وَشُبْهَةٍ

In purification the self expands by the power of the Haqq.
Now do not wonder and ask 'How?' or 'Where?' or 'What?'

وَزَادَتْ بِتَحْمِيلِ الإِلَهِ أَمَانَةً

عَلَيْهَا فَمَا حَدُّ الإِلَهِ تَعَدَّتِ

It expands by Allah's bestowal of the trust upon it
– and godhood has no limitation whatsoever.

وَقَدْ عَجَزَتْ عَنْهَا الْعِظَامُ مِنَ الْوَرَىٰ
وَقَامَ بِهَا الْإِنْسَانُ أَرْفَعَ قَوْمَةِ

Even great men have proved unable to bear this trust,
yet still man has to take it on, and this is the highest task.

فَيَا سَعْدَ مَنْ أَضْحَىٰ يُتَابِعُ سَيِّدًا
رَسُولًا لَهُ أَعْلَا الْمَزَايَا وَرُتْبَةِ

How fulfilled is the one who has begun to follow a master,
a Messenger who has the highest rank and merit,

فَفَازَ مِنَ الْخَيْرَاتِ فَوْقَ نِهَايَةِ
وَأُمَّتُهُ أُرْبَتْ عَلَىٰ كُلِّ أُمَّةِ

For he will gain benefits without end or limit,
and his Community is above every other.

فَلَا أَحَدٌ يَرْقَىٰ لِرُتْبَةِ قُرْبِهِ
وَذَاكَ بِتَخْصِيصِ الْإِلَهِ بِعَطْفَةِ

No one may rise to the rank of His nearness which he enjoys,
since that is a special mark of favour from Allah.

فَلَا كَسْبَ لِلْإِنْسَانِ فِي دَرْكِ غَايَةِ
لِمَا خَصَّهُ الرَّحْمَٰنُ فِي أَصْلِ نَشْأَةِ

There is nothing to be gained by a man trying to reach a place
set aside for the Prophet from the beginning of creation.

عَلَيْهِ صَلَاةُ اللهِ مَا جَآءَ وَارِدٌ

يُبَيِّنُ طُرْقَ الْحَقِّ مَعَ سَوْقِ مِنْحَةِ

May Allah's blessings be upon him as long as someone comes
to make clear the paths of truth and bringing gifts,

وَءَالِهِ وَالْاَصْحَابِ مَعَ كُلِّ مُرْشِدٍ

دَعَا لِطَرِيقِ اللهِ فِي كُلِّ حَالَةِ

and on his family and Companions, and every Murshid
who calls to the Path of Allah in every situation.

وَأَسْأَلُ رَبِّ اللهَ إِلْقَآءَ سِرِّهِ

عَلَيَّ مَعَ الْاِخْوَانِ فِي كُلِّ وِجْهَةِ

I ask my Lord Allah to bestow His secret on me
and on my brothers in every way.

قَدْ وَافَقَتِ الْاِسْمَ الْعَظِيمِ جَلَالَةً

بِعَدِّ فَنَفْسْ فِي افْتِتَاجٍ وَخَتْمَةِ ۞

All this is in harmony with the majesty of the Supreme Name,
and numerically, so pay attention to its beginning and its end.

Lesser Qasida

وله رضي الله عنه ورزقنا في الدارين رضاه آمين
التائية الوسطى

شَرِبْنَا مِنَ الأَنْوَارِ فِي حَانِ حَضْرَةٍ
شَرَابًا أَزَالَ اللَّبْسَ مِنْ غَيْرِ مِرْيَةٍ

In the tavern of the Presence we drank a wine
of the lights that totally dispelled the darkness.

فَأَدْرَكْنَا أَنَّ الْفِعْلَ فِي كُلِّ ذَرَّةٍ
بِخَالِقِهَا الْمَعْبُودِ فِي كُلِّ وِجْهَةٍ

Through it we grasped that the act is in every atom
through its Creator Who is worshipped everywhere.

وَحَقَّقْنَا أَنَّ اللهَ فِي الْكُلِّ ظَاهِرٌ
بِأَسْمَائِهِ الْحُسْنَىٰ وَأَسْرَارِ قُدْرَةٍ

We realised that Allah is manifest in everything
through His most Beautiful Names and the secrets of power.

73

وَلَكِنَّ أَحْوَالَ الْوُجُودِ كَثِيرَةٌ

بِهَا وَقَعَ الْحُجْبُ الْعَظِيمُ لِحِكْمَةِ

However, the states of existence are numerous,
and because of this, great veils have fallen over wisdom.

لِذَا أَرْسَلَ الرَّحْمَنُ خِيرَةَ خَلْقِهِ

بَشِيرًا نَذِيرًا دَاعِيًا بِالْبَصِيرَةِ

Thus the Merciful has sent the flower of His creation
bringing good news and warning, inviting with inner sight.

فَإِنْ شِئْتَ أَنْ تَحْظَىٰ بِنَيْلِ سَعَادَةٍ

فَحَكِّمْهُ تَحْكِيمًا عَلَىٰ كُلِّ خَطْرَةِ

If you wish to obtain the gift of happiness
then make him the guide of your every thought and move.

وَقُلْ لِحُظُوظِ النَّفْسِ لَا تَذْهَبِي مَعِي

وَلَا تَقْطَعِي سَيْرِي لِرَبِّ الْبَرِيَّةِ

Tell the impulses of the self: 'Do not come with me.
Do not cut off my path to the Lord of creation.'

فَمَنْ كَانَ ذَا ذِكْرٍ وَفِكْرٍ وَهِمَّةٍ

تَرَقَّىٰ عَنِ الْأَغْيَارِ فِي كُلِّ لَحْظَةِ

Whoever has got dhikr, fikr and himma
will in every moment transcend otherness.

وَحَازَ مِنَ الْعِرْفَانِ فَوْقَ مُرَادِهِ
وَحَقَّقَ أَسْرَارَ الْوُجُودِ بِسُرْعَةِ

He will attain gnosis beyond his desires
and fast realise the secrets of existence.

وَشَاهَدَ أَنَّ الْفَرْقَ مَحْضُ شَرِيعَةٍ
وَهِيَ عَلَى التَّحْقِيقِ عَيْنُ الحَقِيقَةِ

He will see that separation is the pure Shari'a,
which, properly speaking, is the source of Haqiqa.

لِذَا أَمَرَ الْقُرْءَانُ بِالْفِكْرِ فِي الْوَرَىٰ
وَجَاءَ بِتَوْحِيدٍ مُزِيلٍ لِرِيبَةِ

This is why the Qur'an commands reflection on mankind
which brings a Tawhid that eliminates any doubt.

وَلَيْسَ يُرَى الرَّحْمَـٰنُ إِلَّا فِي مَظْهَرٍ
كَعَرْشٍ وَكُرْسِيٍّ وَلَوْحٍ وَسِدْرَةِ

The Merciful is only to be seen in manifestations
like the Throne, the Footstool, the Tablet, or the Lote-Tree.

وَكُنْهُ صِفَاتِ الرَّبِّ لَيْسَ النُّهَىٰ تَفِي
بِتَحْقِيقِهَا كَشْفًا فَأَحْرَى الْمَهِيَّةِ

The intellect cannot grasp the nature of the Attributes of the Lord
through unveiling, let alone the Essence.

فَكِرَّ عَلَىٰ أَوْصَافِ نَفْسِكَ فَامْحُهَا

تُمَدُّ بِأَنْوَارِ الصِّفَاتِ الْقَدِيمَةِ

So attack the attributes of the self and efface them,
and you will be helped by the lights of the eternal Attributes.

لِذَاكَ تَرَى الْعُشَّاقَ قَدْ ثَمِلُوا بِهَا

وَأَحْسَنُهُمْ سُكْرًا مَلِيكُ الْإِبَاحَةِ

Thus you will see lovers who have become intoxicated by the lights,
and the drunkest lover is the one who is given special licence.

وَلَيْسَ عَلَى الْمَغْلُوبِ مِنْ حَرَجٍ وَلَا

عَلَىٰ أَهْلِ الْإِذْنِ مِنْ وُضُوحِ الْإِشَارَةِ

There is no restriction on the clear ishara those utterly overwhelmed
by Allah may make, nor on the people of Idhn.

فَدُونَكَ قَوْمًا قَدْ أَذَابُوا نُفُوسَهُمْ

نَفَاضُوا بِحَارَ الْحُبِّ فِي كُلِّ لُجَّةِ

Here are ones who have obliterated their selves
and plumbed every depth in the oceans of love.

فَسَلِّمْ لَهُمْ فِيمَا تَرَىٰ مِنْ صَبَابَةٍ

وَرَقْصٍ عَلَىٰ ذِكْرِ الْحَبِيبِ بِنَغْمَةِ

So submit to them for what you see of their ardent love,
and the dancing and singing in their dhikr of the Beloved.

فَلَوْ ذُقْتَ شَيْئًا مِنْ مَعَانِي كَلَامِنَا

لَكُنْتَ مِنَ السُّبَّاقِ فِي كُلِّ حَالَةِ

If you had but tasted something of the meaning of our words,
you would have been one of the foremost in every circumstance.

وَأَغْضَيْتَ يَا أَخِي الْجُفُونَ عَنِ الْقَذَا

وَمَزَّقْتَ أَثْوَابَ الْحَيَا وَالْمَهَابَةِ

And, my brother, you would have borne your troubles patiently,
and you would have rent the robes of shame and self-importance.

وَقُلْتَ لِحَادِي الْقَوْمِ حَبِّبْنَا فِي اسْمِهِ

فَلَا عَارَ فِي ذَاكَ الْحِدَا وَالصَّبَابَةِ

You would have said to the leader of the people, 'Make us love His name!
There is no shame in that song, nor in that love!'

وَلَكِنَّ مَنْ قَدْ صَارَ مِلْكًا لِنَفْسِهِ

تَقَاعَدَ عَنْ أَسْرَارِ تِلْكَ الطَّرِيقَةِ

Unfortunately, whoever becomes subject to his own self
is cut off from the secrets of this path.

فَأَعْدَا عَدُوٍّ فِي الْوَرَىٰ نَفْسُكَ الَّتِي

تُعَطِّلُ عَنْ تَحْقِيقِ فَهْمِ الْحَقِيقَةِ

The most hostile enemy of man is his self,
which hinders him from real understanding of the Haqiqa.

فَكَبِّرْ عَلَى الْاَكْوَانِ إِنْ شِئْتَ وَصْلَهُ

وَإِيَّاكَ أَنْ تَرْضَىٰ بِنَيْلِ الْكَرَامَةِ

So become greater than the common people if you desire to reach Him,
and do not be satisfied with a mere reputation of nobility.

فَيَا فَوْزَ قَوْمٍ قَدْ أَجَابُوا حَبِيبَهُمْ

لِدَعْوَتِهِ الْعُظْمَىٰ فَفَازُوا بِجَنَّةِ

Oh the triumph of a people who have answered
the great call of the Beloved, and so obtained the Garden!

وَأَعْنِي بِهِ الْعِرْفَانَ فِي حَضْرَةِ الدُّنَا

وَجَنَّةِ أَنْهَارٍ وَحُورٍ وَلَذَّةِ

By that I mean both 'irfan in the presence of nearness
and the garden of rivers, houris, and delight.

عَلَىٰ نَفْسِهِ فَلْيَبْكِ مَنْ صَارَ قَلْبُهُ

خَرَابًا مِنَ الْعِرْفَانِ فِي كُلِّ فِكْرَةِ

Let the one whose heart has become devoid and empty
of 'irfan in every thought weep over himself.

وَمَا لَذَّةُ الْعَيْشِ السَّلِيمِ مِنَ النَّغْصِ

وَرَبِّي إِلَّا فِي تَحَقُّقِ وُصْلَةِ

The joy of life without trouble, by my Lord,
is only found in the realisation of reunion.

عَسَىٰ نَظْرَةٌ تَشْفِي السَّقِيمَ مِنَ الضَّنَا

فَقَدْ عَزَّ إِدْرَاكٌ لِكُنْهِ الْحَقِيقَةِ

Perhaps a glance will cure the sick man of his sickness,
for the perception of the essence of Haqiqa is mighty.

فَأَطْيَبُ أَوْقَاتِي اتّصَافِي بِذِلَّةٍ

وَعَجْزٍ وَفَقْرٍ وَانْسِلَابِ إِرَادَةِ

My best time is when I am characterised by humility,
incapacity, poverty, and negation of the will.

فَتِلْكَ أُصُولٌ فِي طَرِيقَتِنَا الْمُثْلَىٰ

فَكُنْهُ وَجِنْبْ عَنْ عُلُوٍّ وَرِفْعَةِ

For these are the foundations of our perfect path.
So follow it and avoid reputation and self-importance.

وَكُلُّ صِفَاتِ الرَّبِّ فَاهْرُبْ لِضِدِّهَا

تَكُونُ بِفَضْلِ اللهِ أَغْنَى الْبَرِيَّةَ

Flee to the opposite of the Attributes of the Lord,
then by Allah's favour, you will be the richest of creation.

فَأَوْصَافُهُ الْعِلْمُ الْمُحِيطُ وَقُدْرَةً

وَأَوْصَافُنَا جَهْلٌ وَعَجْزٌ عَنْ ذَرَّةِ

His Attributes are encompassing knowledge, and power over everything,
and our attributes are ignorance and less power than a particle of dust.

وَإِنْ شِئْتَ قَصْدَ الْعَارِفِينَ بِأَسْرِهِمْ
نُخُذْهُ وَكُنْ يَا صَاحِ صَاحِبَ هِمَّةٍ

If you desire to reach the goal of all the 'Arifeen,
then take it, O my companion, and have himma.

عُبُودِيَّةٌ لِلَّهِ صَادِقَةٌ وَمَعْ
قِيَامٍ بِحَقِّ الرَّبِّ فِي كُلِّ لَحْظَةٍ

Being a slave of Allah is sincere when it goes
along with undertaking the rights of the Lord at every moment.

وَأَعْنِي بِهَا التَّجْرِيدَ مِنْ كُلِّ قُوَّةٍ
وَحَوْلٍ وَأَسْبَابٍ وَنَيْلِ الْمَزِيَّةِ

By slavehood I mean *tajrid* from every power and strength
and any means, and even getting things for yourself.

لِأَنَّ بِهَا يَصْفُو الْفُؤَادُ مِنَ الْعَمَىٰ
وَيَمْلَأُ بِالْأَنْوَارِ فِي كُلِّ فِكْرَةٍ

Because in this way the heart is purified of blindness
and is filled with lights in every thought.

فَقَدْ كُمِّلَتْ وَالْحَمْدُ فِي الْبَدْءِ وَالْخَتْمِ
عَلَىٰ نِعْمَةِ الْإِمْدَادِ مِنْ خَيْرِ أُمَّةٍ

The song is over. Praise is due at the beginning and the end
for the gift of help from the Best of the Community.

عَلَيْهِ صَلَاةُ اللهِ فِي كُلِّ لَحْظَةٍ

وَءَالِهِ وَالْاَصْحَابِ أَهْلِ الْعِنَايَةِ

May the blessings of Allah be upon him at every instant
and his family, and his Companions, the people in Allah's care.

وَنَاظِمُهَا الْمَعْرُوفُ أَعْنِي مُحَمَّدًا

هُوَ ابْنُ حَبِيبٍ طَالِبًا لِلْعبودةِ

Its well-known writer, I mean Muhammad
ibn al-Habib, seeks perfect slavehood.

فَبَلِّغْهُ يَا ذَا الْفَضْلِ مِنْكَ بِنَفْحَةٍ

تَسُحُّ عَلَى الْاَكْوَانِ فَيْضَ الْحَقِيقَةِ ۞

So convey him a fragrance from You, O Master of Generosity,
that will spread the effulgence of Haqiqa over all creation.

Minor Qasida

وتليها

التائية الصغرى

سَقَانِي َ حِبِّي مِنْ صَفَاءِ مَحَبَّةٍ
فَأَصْبَحْتُ مَحْبُوبًا لَدَىٰ كُلِّ نِسْبَةِ

My Beloved gave me a drink of the purest love,
so I became beloved in every way.

وَغَيَّبَنِي عَنِّي فَلَمْ أَرَ غَيْرَهُ
وَنَعَّمَ سِرِّي فِي مَظَاهِرِ حَضْرَةِ

He blinded me to myself so that I saw only Him,
and dissolved my secret in the manifestations of the Presence.

فَفَرَّقْتُ فِي جَمْعِي وَجَمَّعْتُ مَفْرُوقِي
وَحَقَّقْتُ تَوْحِيدِي بِإِفْرَادِ وَحْدَةِ

I separated what was gathered in me and gathered what was separate;
by the isolation of unity I realised my Tawhid.

وَنِلْتُ مُرَادِي مِنْ شُهُودٍ كَمَالِهِ
وَحَقَّقْتُهُ فِي كُلِّ مَعْنًى وَصُورَةِ

I attained my desire – directly to see His perfection
and to experience it in every meaning and form.

وَمَزَّقْتُ وَهْمِي وَهْوَ أَعْظَمُ قَاطِعٍ
فَأَلْفَيْتُهُ قَيُّومًا فِي كُلِّ ذَرَّةِ

I tore down my illusion, which is the greatest screen,
and then I found Him, timeless, in every atom.

وَحَكَّمْتُ شَرْعِي فِي تَجَلِّي صِفَاتِهِ
فَأَطْلَعَنِي رَبِّي عَلَىٰ سِرِّ حِكْمَتِي

I made the Shari'a my guide in taking on His Attributes,
and my Lord revealed to me the secret of my wisdom.

فَطَوْرًا أَرَى الاَكْوَانَ مَظْهَرَ أَحْمَدٍ
وَطَوْرًا أَرَاهَا مِنْ مَظَاهِرِ عِزَّةِ

Sometimes I see creatures as a manifestation of Ahmad,
and sometimes I see them as manifestations of divine Power.

وَطَوْرًا يَفْنَىٰ فِعْلِي بِرُؤْيَةِ فِعْلِهِ
وَطَوْرًا أَرَى الاَوْصَافَ مِنْهُ تَبَدَّتْ

Sometimes my action is obliterated by the sight of His action,
and sometimes I see the Attributes appearing from Him.

وَطَوْرًا أَغِيبُ عَنْ وُجُودٍ مَجَازِيِّ

فِي وَحْدَةِ حَقٍّ لَا تُشَابُ بِشِرْكَةِ

And sometimes I withdraw from metaphorical existence
into the unity of a Truth unmarked by shirk.

وَمَا الْخَلْقُ إِلَّا كَالْهَبَا فِي الْهَوَىٰ لِمَنْ

تَغِيَّبَ فِي أَنْوَارِ ذِكْرِ الْحَقِيقَةِ

To anyone who withdraws into the lights of the dhikr of the Truth,
creation is nothing more than particles of dust in the air.

فَفِي ذِكْرِهَا الْفَتْحُ الْمُبِينُ لِتَائِبِ

تَحَلَّىٰ بِصَبْرٍ مَعَ تَحَقُّقِ نِعْمَةِ

The dhikr of the Truth contains the clear opening for the man of tawba
who has adorned himself with patience and the realisation of benefits.

فَقَامَ بِشُكْرِ اللهِ لِكُلِّ نِعْمَةٍ

تَجَلَّىٰ بِهَا الْوَهَّابُ فِي كُلِّ حَالَةِ

He has thus undertaken to show gratitude to Allah in every state
for every gift by which the Giver manifests Himself.

فَأَوْرَثَهُ حُبُّ التَّفَرُّدِ دَائِمًا

تَحَقُّقَ إِمْدَادٍ أَتَتْ بِسَكِينَةِ

The love of isolation grants him continual realisation
of aid which comes with the Sakina.

فَصَارَ يُحِبُّ اللهَ حَقًّا بِلَا رَيْبٍ

لِرُؤْيَتِهِ الْاِحْسَانَ فِي كُلِّ لَحْظَةٍ

He will begin to love Allah truly, without doubt,
since he witnesses Ihsan at every instant.

فَكُلُّ مَقَامَاتِ الْيَقِينِ قَدِ انْطَوَتْ

فِي صَبْرٍ وَحُبٍّ خَالِصٍ مِنْ مَشُوبَةٍ

Firm patience and untarnished, pure love
indeed contain all the Stations of Certainty.

وَلَا بُدَّ فِي ذَا مِنْ إِمَامٍ لِسَالِكٍ

يَدُلُّ عَلَى بِرٍّ وَتَقْوَىٰ وَسُنَّةٍ

To obtain these the Salik must have an Imam
to guide him in right action, taqwa and Sunna.

وَدَعْ عَنْكَ مَحْجُوبًا غَفُولًا عَنْ رَبِّهِ

جَهُولًا بِطُرْقِ اللهِ مِنْ فَرْطِ ظُلْمَةٍ

Leave alone the one who is veiled, unaware of his Lord,
and in his deep inner darkness utterly ignorant of the Paths of Allah.

وَإِيَّاكَ أَنْ تَرْضَىٰ بِصُحْبَةِ فِرْقَةٍ

تَمَكَّنَ مِنْهَا الشَّرُّ فِي كُلِّ قَوْلَةٍ

Beware of ending up satisfied to be in the company
of a sect whom evil masters in their every word,

يَقُولُونَ بِالْأَفْوَاهِ مَا لَيْسَ فِي الْحَشَا

وَيَاتُونَ مِنْ أَفْعَالٍ كُلِّ قَبِيحَةِ

Saying with their mouths what is not in their hearts,
while at the same time doing every revolting act.

نَصَحْتُكَ بَعْدَ الْبَحْثِ إِنْ كُنْتَ سَامِعًا

فَمَا الدِّينُ إِلَّا نُصْحُ كُلِّ الْخَلِيقَةِ

I have counselled you after investigation if you will only listen,
for the Deen is only giving every person good counsel.

فَكَمْ قَدْ أَزَاغُوا مِنْ عُقُولٍ بَسِيطَةٍ

خَلَتْ عَنْ تَوْفِيقِ نُورِ رَبِّ الْبَرِيَّةِ

How many simple minds have got lost because they lacked
the guidance of the light of the Lord of creation?

وَقَدْ صَارَتِ الْأَعْرَاضُ فِي هَتْكِهَا لَهُمْ

قَبَائِحُ أَغْرَاضٍ هِيَ شَرُّ فِتْنَةِ

Their original good name has been debased and disgraced
falling into the worst temptation, ugly deeds of shame.

وَقَدْ أَمَرَ الشَّرْعُ الْمُبِينُ بِتَعْظِيمِ

لِمَنْ كَانَ ذَا نَفْعٍ بِإِرْشَادِ أُمَّةِ

The clear Shari'a commands that we honour and esteem,
whoever has the best guidance for the Community.

وَطُوبَىٰ لِمَشْغُولٍ بِتَهْذِيبِ نَفْسِهِ
يُجَاهِدُهَا بِالذِّكْرِ فِي كُلِّ حَالَةِ

Bliss belongs to the one occupied with correction of the self,
who struggles against it with dhikr in every State,

وَيَتْلُو كِتَابَ اللهِ بِالْجِدِّ دَائِمًا
وَيَقْتَبِسُ الْأَنْوَارَ مِنْ كُلِّ ءَايَةِ

who constantly reads the Book of Allah with gravity,
and who seeks the knowledge of lights from every ayat,

يُحَكِّمُهُ فِي كُلِّ مَا هُوَ فَاعِلٌ
وَيَتْبَعُ أَخْلَاقًا لِخَيْرِ الْخَلِيقَةِ

taking it as his judgment in all that he does,
and following the behaviour of the Best of the Community.

فَهُوَ الصِّرَاطُ الْمُسْتَقِيمُ لِمَنْ دَرَا
وَهُوَ الَّذِي أَتَىٰ بِأَفْضَلِ مِلَّةِ

He is the Straight Path for those who understand,
and he is the one who has brought the fullest of spiritual teachings.

عَلَيْهِ صَلَاةُ اللهِ مَعْ ءَالِهِ وَمَنْ
تَلَاهُمْ بِإِحْسَانٍ إِلَىٰ يَوْمِ بَعْثَةِ ۞

May Allah's blessings always be upon him and his family
and whoever follows them with Ihsan until the Day of Rising.

Doctrines of Tawhid

ويليها رجز
عقائد التوحيد

يَقُولُ عَبْدُ رَبِّهِ رَبَّهُ مُحَمَّدُ
إِبْنُ الْحَبِيبِ رَبَّهُ يُوَحِّدُ

The slave of his Lord, Muhammad ibn al-Habib,
says, declaring the absolute oneness of his Lord:

بِاسْمِ الإِلَهِ فِي الأُمُورِ أَشْرَعُ
إِلَيْهِ بَدْؤُهَا كَذَاكَ الْمَرْجَعُ

I begin all things with the 'Bismillah' –
to Him belong their beginning as well as their returning.

مَعْنَى الإِلَهِ الْغَنِي عَنْ سِوَاهُ
وَلَهُ يَفْتَقِرُ مَا عَدَاهُ

The meaning of 'god' is That which has no need of other-than-Him,
while anything other has need of Him.

لِلِاسْتِغْنَىٰ عَنْ كُلِّ مَا سِوَاهُ

يَجِ مِنَ الأوْصَافِ لَا تَنْسَاهُ

This 'That' which has no need of other-than-Him
possesses thirteen Attributes, do not forget it!

وُجُودٌ ثُمَّ قِدَمٌ ثُمَّ الْبَقَا

مُخَالَفَهْ ثُمَّ غِنَاهُ مُطْلَقَا

Existence, then pre-existence, then going-on,
being different from creation, then His absolute independence.

وَالسَّمْعُ وَالْبَصَرُ وَالْكَلَامُ

وَالْكَوْنُ لَازِمٌ لَهَا أَحْكَامُ

Hearing, sight and speech
and the fact that there are rulings inherent in them.

وَعَدَمُ الأغْرَاضِ فِي الأفْعَالِ

كَذَاكَ فِي الأَحْكَامِ رُدَّ الْبَالِ

Acts devoid of motive or need,
and similarly judgments; pay attention.

جَوَازُ فِعْلِ ثُمَّ تَرْكِ أَلْحَقَا

بِمَا ذَكَرْنَاهُ وَكُنْ مُحَقَّقَا

Total freedom of action and of non-action
– connect to what we have told you and realise it!

وَلَافْتِقَارِ كُلِّ مَا عَدَاهُ

يَبُّ مِنَ الْأَوْصَافِ مُنْتَهَاهُ

The poverty of all that is other-than-Him
has in the end twelve attributes:

اَلْعِلْمُ وَالْقُدْرَةُ وَالْارَادَهْ

ثُمَّ الْحَيَاةُ حَقِّقِ الْافَادَهْ

Knowledge, power, and will,
then life – grasp the lesson intended here!

زِدْ قَادِرًا وَمُرِيدًا وَعَالِمْ

حَيًّا فَلَا تَكْتَفِي بِاللَّوَازِمْ

In addition He is Capable, Willing, Knowing
Living – but do not be content with the inherent attributes.

وَحْدَةُ فِعْلٍ وَ كَذَا وَصْفٍ وَذَاتْ

بِنَفْيِ كَمِّ فَاسْئَلَنْ عَنْهَا الثِّقَاتْ

Unity of action, attribute and essence
with rejection of quantity – ask trustworthy ones about it.

حُدُوثُ عَالَمٍ وَنَفْيُ تَاثِيرِ

بِطَبْعٍ أَوْ بِقُوَّةٍ فَاعْتَبِرِ

The originated nature of the universe and the negation
of effect either by nature or by a faculty – so take note.

90

$$\text{فَتِلْكَ خَمْسَةٌ وَعِشْرُونَ صِفَه}$$

$$\text{وَالضِّدُّ مِثْلُهَا فَفَصِّلْ عَدَدَه}$$

These are twenty-five attributes.
Their opposites are the same in number – count them.

$$\text{وَلِلْإِيمَانِ بِالرَّسُولِ عَشَرَه}$$

$$\text{وَسِتَّةٌ مِنَ الصِّفَاتِ تَابِعَه}$$

Belief in the Messenger
has sixteen attributes which are:

$$\text{اَلصِّدْقُ وَالتَّبْلِيغُ وَالأَمَانَه}$$

$$\text{وَجَوَازُ الأَعْرَاضِ لِلْإِفَادَه}$$

Truthfulness, conveyance of the message and trustworthiness,
the conceivability of being subject to accidents that have meaning.

$$\text{وَإِيمَانٌ بِكُتُبٍ وَأَنْبِيَا}$$

$$\text{وَرُسُلٍ وَأَمْلَاكِ يَا ذَكِيَا}$$

Belief in the Books and the Prophets,
and the Messengers, and the Angels, O man of intellect!

$$\text{وَإِيمَانٌ بِيَوْمِ الآخِرِ فَعْ}$$

$$\text{أَضْدَادَهَا وَكُنْ لِنَفْيِهَا سَاعِي}$$

And belief that the Last Day must come.
Be aware of their opposites and struggle to reject them.

فَتِلْكَ سِتَّةٌ وَسِتُّونَ صِفَه

تَدْخُلُ فِي الْكَلِمَةِ الْمُشَرَّفَه

These are sixty-six Attributes
which are contained in the noble phrase.

فَاشْغَلْ بِهَا الْاَوْقَاتَ بِالْحُضُورِ

تَرْقَ إِلَى الْمَعْنَى مَعَ السُّرُورِ

So occupy your Awqat with them in the Presence,
and joyfully you will rise to their meaning.

دَلِيلُهَا النَّظَرُ فِي الْقُرْءَانِ

وَجَوَلَانُ الْعَقْلِ فِي الْاَكْوَانِ

Their proof lies in contemplation of the Qur'an
and in reflecting on created beings with the intellect.

يَا رَبَّنَا صَلِّ عَلَى مُحَمَّدٍ

وَءَالِهِ وَكُلِّ عَبْدٍ مُقْتَدِى

O our Lord, bless Muhammad, and his family
and every slave of Allah who copies him.

وَانْفَعْ بِهَا يَا رَبِّ كُلَّ مَنْ قَرَا

وَسَامِعٍ وَأُمِّيٍّ وَمَنْ دَرَى

And, O Lord, let the educated and the unlettered,
whoever reads or hears this, benefit from these attributes.

وَانْصُرْ أَمِيرَنَا بِخَرْقِ الْعَادَه

وَاحْفَظْ أَنْجَالَهُ وَكُلَّ الْعَائِلَه

And help our Amir with the breaking of norms
and preserve his descendants and all of his family.

وَاجْعَلْهُ عَيْنًا مِنْ عُيُونِ اللهِ

يَنْفَعُ فِي كُلِّ بِلَادِ اللهِ

And make him one of the springs of Allah
who will bring benefit in all the lands of Allah.

وَوَالِ مَنْ وَلَاهُ بِالْاِحْسَانِ

وَمَنْ أَعَانَهُ بِلَا خِذْلَانِ

And befriend whoever befriends him with Ihsan
and whoever helps him without forsaking him.

وَاجْعَلْ لَهُ مِنْ عُلَمَاءِ الْأُمَّه

مَنْ يُخْلِصُ النُّصْحَ لَهُ وَالنِّيَّه

And appoint for him of the 'ulama of the Community
those who are sincere in counsel and intention towards him.

وَوَفِّقِ الْوُلَاةَ لِلْمُسَاعَده

لِكُلِّ مَا فِيهِ صَلَاحُ الْعَمَلَه

Grant success to the leaders who help
in everything in which there is good for the people.

وَاخْتِمْ لَنَا يَا رَبِّ بِالسَّعَادَه

وَارْفُقْ بِنَا عِنْدَ قِيَامِ السَّاعَه ﴿﴾

And grant us a seal, O Lord, of serenity
– and be kind to us when the Hour arrives.

Buraq of the Tariq

ويليه رجز
براق الطريق

يَقُولُ أَفْقَرُ الْوَرىٰ مُحَمَّدُ
إِبْنُ الْحَبِيبِ قَوْلَهُ مُسَدَّدُ

The poorest of mankind, Muhammad
ibn al-Habib, speaking plainly, says:

اَلْحَمْدُ لِلّٰهِ الَّذِي بِخَيْرِهِ
عَمَّ الْوَرىٰ فِي بَرِّهِ وَبَحْرِهِ

Praise belongs to Allah through Whose generosity
mankind has spread over land and sea.

وَأَرْسَلَ الرُّسُلَ بِالشَّرَائِعْ
وَمُعْجِزَاتٍ مَا لَهَا مِنْ دَافِعْ

He sent the Messengers, each with a Shari'a
and miracles which cannot be refuted.

فَلُبُّهَا تَصَوُّفٌ مُحَرَّرٌ

عَلَىٰ كِتَابٍ سُنَّةٍ مُقَرَّرٌ

And its core is Sufism based exactly
and established on the Book and the Sunna.

فَهَاكَ مِنْهَا نُبْذَةً تَقَرِّبُ

طَرِيقَهُ وَسَيْرَهُ تُحَبِّبُ

Here is a fragment of it which will bring His path close
and make its journeying precious and dear to you.

سَمَّيْتُهَا بِبُرَاقِ الطَّرِيقِ

تُسْرِعُ بِالْمُرِيدِ لِلتَّحْقِيقِ

I have named it 'The Buraq of the Tariq'
for it will bring the murid swiftly to realisation.

فَإِنْ تُرِدْ سُلُوكَكَ الطَّرِيقَا

فَاعْتَمِدِ اللهَ وَسَلْ تَوْفِيقَا

If you wish to take Suluk on the Path,
then rely on Allah and ask Him for success.

وَأَرِحِ النَّفْسَ مِنَ التَّدْبِيرِ

فَإِنَّ ذَا يَجْلُبُ لِلتَّنْوِيرِ

Relieve the self of management,
for that will bring enlightenment.

إِيَّاكَ أَنْ تَهْتَمَّ بِالْاَرْزَاقِ

لِاَنَّهَا فِي ضَمَانِ الْخَلَّاقِ

Beware of anxiety about your means of living,
for that is the responsibility of the Creator.

وَخَصْلَتَانِ لَيْسَ شَيْءٌ يُوجَدُ

فَوْقَهُمَا مِنَ الْخَيْرَاتِ يُحْمَدُ

The highest and most praiseworthy qualities
are contained in these two good practices:

حُسْنُ ظَنٍّ بِاللهِ ثُمَّ بِالْعِبَادْ

فَكُنْ هُمَا وَجَنِّبَنَّ لِلْعِنَادْ

Think the best of Allah and then think the best of His slaves.
Hold to these two things and avoid being wilful.

وَأَقْرَبُ الطُّرُقِ عِنْدَ اللهِ

أَنْ تُكْثِرَ الذِّكْرَ بِإِسْمِ اللهِ

The closest path which leads to Allah
is frequent dhikr of the Name of Allah,

لِأَنَّهُ الاِسْمُ الْعَظِيمُ الاَعْظَمُ

عَلَى الاَصَحِّ مِنْ خِلَافٍ يُعْلَمُ

Because it is the sublime and Supreme Name,
according to the most sound of the different points of view.

وَفَرِّغِ الْقَلْبَ مِنَ الاَغْيَارِ
عِنْدَ التَّوجُّهِ لِذِكْرِ الْبَارِي

Completely free the heart of all otherness
when you turn to the dhikr of the Creator.

وَانْظُرْ لِأَسْرَارِ الْحَكِيمِ وَاعْتَبَرْ
وَجَنِّبِ الْخَوْضَ وَلَا تَكُنْ تُصِرّ

Look at the secrets of the All-Wise and take note.
Avoid plunging into them. Do not persist.

بَلْ عَقِّبِ الذَّنْبَ بِالِاسْتِغْفَارِ
وَبِالتَّضَرُّعِ وَالانْكِسَارِ

Rather, after your wrong action you must ask forgiveness
with contrite entreaty and regret.

وَانْظُرْ لِمَا مَنَّ بِهِ عَلَيْكَا
مِنْ كُلِّ طَاعَةٍ سَعَتْ إِلَيْكَا

Look to Him and grasp that every act in which you obey Him
is, in fact, a gift which He gave to you.

وَاحْمَدهُ فِي السَّرَّاءِ وَالضَّرَّاءِ
لِأَنَّهُ الْفَاعِلُ فِي الاَشْيَاءِ

Praise Him whether things go well or go badly,
because He is the Actor in everything.

وَحَرِّكِ الْهِمَّةَ بِالاَشْوَاقِ

وَلَا تَكُنْ تَرْضَىٰ بِدُونِ الْبَاقِي

Awaken your himma with yearning and longing,
and do not be content with less than the Ever-Continuing.

وَلَا تَقِفْ مَعَ الْبَوَارِقِ وَلَا

مَعْ غَيْرِهَا مِنْ كُلِّ شَيْءٍ حَصَلَا

Do not stop just at the first gleams,
nor with anything else you may experience at this stage.

وَاسْأَلْهُ أَنْ يَطْوِي لَكَ الطَّرِيقَا

حَتَّىٰ تَذُوقَ ذَٰلِكَ التَّحْقِيقَا

Ask Him to let you cover the path with speed
until you fully taste that realisation.

فَاللهُ يَجْتِي مِنَ الْعَبِيدِ

مَنْ شَاءَهُ لِحَضْرَةِ التَّفْرِيدِ

Allah chooses whomever He wants from among His slaves
for the Presence of Isolation.

إِيَّاكَ أَنْ تَسْتَبْعِدَ الطَّرِيقَا

فَإِنَّ ذَا يُكْسِبُكَ التَّعْوِيقَا

Take care you do not consider the path too long,
since that will just become an obstruction for you.

وَاسْلُكْ بِنَفْسِكَ سَبِيلَ الرِّفْقِ

لِكَيْ يَكُونَ سَيْرُهَا بِالشَّوْقِ

Travel with your nafs the way of gentleness
so that you may travel the path with yearning.

فَإِنَّ رَكْعَتَيْنِ مِنْ مُحِبٍّ

أَفْضَلُ مِنْ أَلْفٍ مِنْ غَيْرِ حُبٍّ

Indeed, two rak'ats from a lover are more excellent
than a thousand performed without love.

وَالأَدَبَ اجْعَلْنَهُ رَفِيقَا

فِي أَخْذِكَ التَّشْرِيعَ وَالتَّحْقِيقَا

Make adab your companion as you follow the Shari'a,
and as you recognise the Haqiqa.

فَمَثَلُ الأَدَبِ فِي الأُمُورِ

كَخَلْطِكَ الْحَدِيدَ بِالإِكْسِيرِ

The mithal of adab in these matters
is like mixing iron with elixir.

أَمَا تَرَاهُ يَقْلِبُ الْحَدِيدَا

فِي لَحْظَةٍ بِذَهَبٍ جَدِيدَا

Do you not see how it turns the iron
in an instant to new gold?

كَذَٰلِكَ الاَدَبُ لِلْقُلُوبِ

يَنْقُلُهَا لِحَضْرَةِ الْغُيُوبِ

In the same way adab acts on the heart
and carries it to the Presence of the Unseen.

فَكَمْ مُجِدٍّ عَمَلًا قَدْ وَكَّلَهْ

لِنَفْسِهِ وَكَمْ أَدِيبٍ قَرَّبَهْ

How many a man of earnest right actions He has left to himself,
and how many men of adab He has brought near.

فَأَدَبُ النَّظَرِ فِي الاَكْوَانْ

شُهُودُ بَارِيهَا بِغَيْرِ ثَانْ

The adab of looking at created beings
is that you see the Creator – no second!

فَتُبْصِرُ الْخَالِقَ فِي الْمَخْلُوقِ

وَتُبْصِرُ الرَّازِقَ فِي الْمَرْزُوقِ

Thus you discern the Creator in the created
and the Provider in the provision.

وَالْحَقُّ لَا يُرَىٰ فِي غَيْرِ مَظْهَرٍ

لِأَحَدٍ مِنْ مَلَكٍ أَوْ بَشَرٍ

The Haqq can only be seen in manifestation,
whether by an angel or a mortal man.

فَالْمَظْهَرُ الأَوَّلُ نُورُ أَحْمَدَا

عَلَيْهِ أَفْضَلُ الصَّلَاةِ سَرْمَدَا

The first manifestation is the light of Ahmad,
may the most excellent of blessings be upon him eternally.

قَدْ مَلَأَ الْحَقُّ بِهِ الأَكْوَانَا

وَكُلَّ مَا يَكُونُ أَوْ قَدْ كَانَا

By him the Haqq has filled every living creature
as well as all that is or was.

فَاشْهَدْهُ فِي النَّفْسِ وَفِي الآفَاقِ

وَامْزُجْ بِذَلِكَ رُؤْيَةَ الْخَلَّاقِ

So see him in the self and on the horizon,
and join to that perception of the Creator.

تُكْفَى بِذَا الشُّهُودِ كُلَّ عَيْبٍ

فِي النَّفْسِ وَالْقَلْبِ وَغَيْبِ الْغَيْبِ

And that seeing will compensate for every defect
in the self, the heart, and the unseen of the unseen.

وَذَكِّرِ النَّفْسَ بِحُسْنِ نِيَّةٍ

وَاقْرِنْهَا بِالسُّكُونِ وَالْحَرَكَةِ

Remind the self by having a good niyyat,
and bind it to that in stillness and in movement.

وَنِمِهَا تَنْمِيَةً وَكَثِّرًا

لَهَا تَحُوزُ فَضْلَهَا بِلَا مِرَا

Foster its growth a great deal,
and you will undoubtedly gain a great gift for it.

وَاخْتَصِرِ الطَّرِيقَ بِالتَّعْظِيمِ

لِكُلِّ مَا شُرِعَ مِنْ مَرْسُومِ

Shorten the Tariqa by showing honour and respect
for all that is laid down as the Shari'a.

وَلَا تَكُنْ تَحْقِرْ مِنَ الأَعْمَالِ

شَيْئًا أَتَىٰ وَلَا مِنَ الأَقْوَالِ

Make sure you do not scorn any deeds or words
that have been passed down to us.

طَرِيقَةُ الأَبْدَالِ جُوعٌ سَهَرٌ

صَمْنٌ وَعُزْلَةٌ وَذِكْرٌ حَرَّرُوا

The Tariqa of the Abdal is hunger, sleeplessness,
silence, withdrawal and dhikr. They give freedom.

قَدِ انْتَهَتْ نُبْذَةٌ ذَا التَّصَوُّفِ

وَالْحَمْدُ لِلَّهِ عَلَى التَّعَرُّفِ

This fragment of Sufism is ended
and praise belongs to Allah for the knowledge of it.

وَأُصَلِّي عَلَى النَّبِيِّ الْمُمِدِّ
صَلَاةَ رَبِّنَا بِغَيْرِ حَدِّ

I ask for the limitless blessings of our Lord
on the Prophet, the Helper.

وَءَالِهِ وَصَحْبِهِ الثِّقَاتِ
اَلسَّالِكِينَ سُبُلَ النَّجَاةِ

And on his family and trustworthy Companions,
the wayfarers who trod the paths of safety.

وَأَسْأَلُ اللهَ صَلَاحَ الْحَالِ
لَنَا وَلِلْاَحْبَابِ فِي الْمَئَآلِ

I ask Allah to give us and our loved ones
a sound state in the future.

وَأَنْ يُزِيلَ عَنَّا كُلَّ رَيْبٍ
بِجَاهِ كُلِّ عَارِفٍ مُرَبِّي

And that He remove every doubt from us,
by the rank of every teaching 'Arif.

وَالْحَمْدُ لِلَّهِ عَلَى التَّمَامِ
وَالشُّكْرُ لِلَّهِ عَلَى انْخِتَامِ ۞

Praise is to due to Allah for its completion
and thanks is due to Allah for its seal.

Miracles of the Way

وَيَلِيه رجز

خوارق الطريق

اَلْحَمْدُ لِلَّهِ وَصَلَّى اللهُ
عَلَى النَّبِيّ مُحَمَّدُ الاوَّاهُ

Praise belongs to Allah. May Allah bless
the Prophet Muhammad, the Shelter.

قَالَ أَبُو حَامِدٍ الصُّوفِيُّ
حُجَّةُ الاسْلَامِ هُوَ الطُّوسِيُّ

Abu Hamid at-Tusi, the Sufi
and proof of Islam, said:

كَرَامَةُ الدَّاخِلِ فِي الطَّرِيقِ
عِشْرُونَ فِي الدُّنْيَا عَلَى التَّحْقِيقِ

The marks of honour for the one who enters
the Tariq are twenty in number:

أَوَّلُهَا يَذْكُرُهُ الإِلَهُ
كَمَا يَلِيقُ بِهِ يَا بُشْرَاهُ

The first of them is that Allah remembers him
as is fitting. Oh what good news that is!

ثَانِيهَا تَعْظِيمُهُ بَيْنَ الأَنَامْ
وَالثَّالِثُ الْحُبُّ لَهُ بِلَا مَلَامْ

The second sign is that he is exalted among people,
and the third is a love which finds no reproach.

وَكُلُّ مَنْ أَحَبَّهُ الإِلَهُ
أَحَبَّهُ الْخَلْقُ فَيَا سَعْدَاهُ

And everyone Allah loves, is loved by the creation
– what good fortune he gains!

رَابِعُهَا يُدَبِّرُ الأُمُورَا
لَهُ فَيَبْقَى دَائِمًا مَسْرُورَا

The fourth is that Allah directs all his affairs,
so he remains constantly full of joy.

خَامِسُهَا تَسْهِيلُهُ الرِّزْقَ لَهُ
بِلَا مَشَقَّةٍ فِيهِ تَلْحَقُهُ

The fifth is that Allah makes his food easy to get,
and he does not have to struggle to get it.

سَادِسُهَا يَنصُرُهُ عَلَى الْعِدَا

بِخَرْقِ عَادَةٍ مَعْ حِفْظٍ أَبَدَا

The sixth is that He helps him against his enemies
by miracles, with constant protection.

سَابِعُهَا يَكُونُ أُنْسَهُ فَلَا

وَحْشَةَ تَاتِيهِ مِنْ شَيْءٍ نَزَلَا

The seventh is intimacy with Allah,
so he is never lonely whatever happens.

ثَامِنُهَا الْعِزُّ لَهُ فِي النَّفْسِ

فَالْكَوْنُ يَخْدِمُهُ دُونَ لَبْسِ

The eighth is his nobility of self,
so that creation serves him without confusion.

تَاسِعُهَا الرَّفْعُ لِهِمَّةٍ لَهُ

عَنْ كُلِّ شَيْءٍ فَاتِنٍ يَشْغَلُهُ

The ninth is the elevation of his Himma
above every temptation that might obsess him.

عَاشِرُهَا الْغِنَى لِقَلْبِهِ مَعَ

تَسْهِيلِ أَمْرِهِ الَّذِي فِيهِ سَعَى

The tenth sign is his heart's freedom from need,
along with every matter he strives for being made easy.

وَهَاكَ بَاقِيهَا مَعَ اخْتِصَارِ

بِعَطْفِ بَعْضِهَا نَخُذْ يَا قَارِي

Here briefly follow the rest of them,
stressing only some of them, so attend, O reader!

تَنْوِيرُ قَلْبٍ يَهْتَدِي بِنُورِهِ

لِفَهْمِ أَسْرَارٍ بِفَضْلِ رَبِّهِ

Enlightenment of the heart by whose light he is guided
to an understanding of secrets through the gift of his Lord.

وَشَرْحُ صَدْرِهِ فَلَا يَهْتَمْ

بِكُلِّ مِحْنَةٍ بِهِ تَلَمّ

And the expansion of his breast so that
he is undisturbed by whatever trouble befalls him.

مَهَابَةٌ لَهُ وَحُسْنُ مَوْقِعِ

فِي نُفُوسِ النَّاسِ بِغَيْرِ دَافِعِ

He possesses dignity as well as unquestioned
good standing in the hearts of people.

تَحْبِيبُهُ لِكُلِّ خَلْقٍ فِي الْوَرَىٰ

بِوَعْدِ رَبِّنَا لَهُ بِلَا مِرَا

He is made beloved to every single human creature
through the undoubted promise he has from our Lord.

تَبَرُّكٌ بِهِ مَعَ الآدَابِ

مَعَهُ وَلَوْ نُقِلَ لِلتُّرَابِ

People seek baraka from him along with proper adab
towards him, even after he has turned to dust.

تَسْخِيرُهُ الأَرْضَ لَهُ فَيَذْهَبُ

حَيْثُ يَشَا بِسُرْعَةٍ لَا يَرْهَبُ

The earth is subjected to him so that he may go
with speed and without fear wherever he wishes.

وَالْبَرُّ وَالْبَحْرُ مَعَ الْهَوَاءِ

خَادِمَةٌ لَهُ بِلَا امْتِرَاءِ

The land, the sea and the air
are his servants without doubt.

وَحُوشٌ ثُمَّ سِبَاعٌ مَعَ الْهَوَامّ

سَخَّرَهَا الرَّبُّ لَهُ عَلَى الدَّوَامْ

The wild animals, the beasts of prey and the reptiles
have all been subjugated to him by the Lord forever.

مَفَاتِيحُ الْكُنُوزِ وَالْمَعَادِنْ

تَطْلُبُهُ وَهُوَ عَنْهَا بَائِنْ

And the keys of treasures and mines
offer themselves to him, but he has no need.

تَوَسُّلُ النَّاسِ بِجَاهِهِ إِلَى
إِلَهِهِ فِي كُلِّ شَيْءٍ تَزَلَا

By means of his rank, people seek to draw nearer to Allah
in everything that happens.

فَيَقْضِيهِ الرَّبُّ بِلَا تَعْسِيرِ
بِفَضْلِهِ الْمَصْحُوبِ بِالتَّيْسِيرِ

So the Lord accomplishes that without hardship
by His bounty accompanied by ease.

وَذَاكَ مَوْكُولٌ إِلَى إِخْتِيَارِ
إِلَهِهِ فِي سَابِقِ الاقْدَارِ

That has been left to the choice of his God
in His previously ordained decrees.

فَلَا تَقُلْ دَعْوته فَلَمْ يُجِبْ
فَذَاكَ شَأْنُ كُلِّ غَافِلٍ مُرِيبْ

So do not say, 'I called on Him and He did not respond.'
That is the condition of the doubters and the heedless.

أَمَّا الْكَرَامَةُ لَهُ فِي الآخِرَةْ
عِشْرُونَ أَيْضًا هَاكَهَا مُتَّبَعه

As for the marks of honour which he has in the Akhira,
they are also twenty in number and they follow here.

تَسْهِيلُ مَوْتِهِ مَعَ انْخِتَامٍ

عَلَى الايمَانِ فَازَ بِالْمَرَامِ

Ease of death when the seal is set with Iman
so that he will get what he wants.

تَبْشِيرُهُ بِالرَّوْحِ وَالرَّيْحَانْ

وَالامْنِ مِنْ خَوْفٍ مَعَ الرِّضْوَانْ

The good news of cool refreshment, sweet basil,
acceptance, and safety from fear,

كَذَا الْخُلُودُ فِي الْجِنَانِ أَبَدَا

فِي جِوَارِ الرَّحْمٰنِ دَأْبًا سَرْمَدَا

and abiding in the Gardens forever,
near to the All-Merciful, perpetually without end.

لِرُوحِهِ الْعُرُوجُ وَالاِكْرَامُ

مِنَ الْمَلَائِكَةِ وَالانْعَامُ

His ruh enjoys ascent and honour
and tribute from the angels and bliss.

وَالنَّاسُ تَزْدَحِمُ لِلصَّلَاةِ

عَلَيْهِ إِذْ كَانَ مِنَ الثِّقَاتِ

People will crowd around to pray over him
as had been among those worthy of trust.

يُلَقَّنُ الصَّوَابَ فِي السُّؤَالِ

فَلَا يَخَافُ شِدَّةَ الاَهْوَالِ

He will be taught what is correct when asked,
so that he will not fear the severe terrors.

تَوْسِعَةُ القَبْرِ لَهُ فِي رَوْضَةٍ

يَكُونُ فِيهَا ءَامِنًا مِنْ فِتْنَةٍ

The expanse of his grave is in a meadow,
where he will be safe from every trial.

وَإِينَاسٌ لِرُوحِهِ وَجِسْمِهِ

إِذْ تَأْتِيهِ البُشْرَىٰ لَهُ مِنْ رَبِّهِ

When the good news comes to him from his Lord
both his ruh and his body will enjoy intimacy.

تَحْمِلُهُ الطُّيُورُ فِي أَجْوَافِهَا

فِي جَنَّةٍ حَيْثُ يَشَا فِي عَرْضِهَا

Birds will carry him within them
wherever he wishes to roam in the Garden.

وَالْحَشْرُ فِي الْعِزِّ مَعَ الْكَرَامَهْ

وَالتَّاجِ وَالْحُلَلِ وَالشَّفَاعَهْ

On the Day of Gathering, he will be glorified
with honour, a crown, robes of honour and intercession.

بيَاضُ وَجْهِهِ وَنُورُهُ ظَهَرْ

لِكُلِّ مَنْ بِمَوْقِفٍ قَدِ انْتَشَرْ

His face will be radiantly white and its light
will be manifest to all those gathered at the place of standing.

وَهَوْلُ مَوْقِفٍ فَلَا يَرَاهُ

وَالآخِذُ الْكُتْبَ لَهُ يُمْنَاهُ

He will not see the terror of the place where they stand,
and he will receive his book in his right hand.

فَلَا يُحَاسَبُ حِسَابَ عُنْفِ

بَلْ يُبْتَدَى بِجَمِيلٍ وَلُطْفِ

It will not be with severity that he is called to account
but rather it will begin with kindness and gentleness.

أَعْمَالُهُ تُثْقَلُ عِنْدَ الْوَزْنِ

وَالشُّرْبُ مِنْ حَوْضٍ نَبِيٍّ يُغْنِي

His deeds will weigh heavily in the balance
and he will drink from the basin of a Prophet who satisfies every thirst.

جَوَازُهُ الصِّرَاطَ بِالاسْرَاعِ

لِجَنَّةِ الْخُلْدِ بِلَا نِزَاعِ

He will cross the Sirat swiftly without struggle
to reach the Garden of timelessness.

فَلَا يُحَاسَبُ وَلَا يُلَامُ

فِي مَوْقِفِ الْمِيزَانِ لَا يُضَامُ

He will not be called to account for his actions or rebuked,
and in the place of weighing them he will not be harmed.

يَشْفَعُ فِي الْأَهْلِ وَفِي الْإِخْوَانِ

وَيُكْتَسَىٰ مِنْ حُلَلِ الرِّضْوَانِ

He will intercede for his family and the brothers,
and he will be clothed in the robes of serene contentment.

ثُمَّ لِقَاءُ اللهِ بِالْمُعَايِنَه

مِنْ غَيْرِ تَكْيِيفٍ وَلَا مُشَابَهَه

Then he will meet Allah with actual vision
and without qualification or resemblance.

وَهْيَ أَجَلُّ مِنْ دُخُولِ الْجَنَّه

كَمَا أَتَىٰ فِي كِتَابٍ وَسُنَّه

That will be more glorious than entering the Garden,
as it says in the Book and the Sunna.

وَشَرْطُ مَنْ يَمْنَحُهُ الْإِلَهُ

بِهَذِهِ الْخُلَعِ لَا تَنْسَاهُ

Take care not to forget that Allah's granting
of these robes of honour is conditional —

اَلْعِلْمُ وَالْعَمَلُ مَعْ إِخْلَاصٍ

وَالذِّكْرُ يُؤْذِنُ بِالاِخْتِصَاصِ

On knowledge, actions of Ikhlas
and the dhikr which indicates his special place.

فَغَايَةُ الطَّرِيقِ فِي اسْتِغْرَاقِ

فِي شُهُودٍ لِمَالِكٍ خَلَّاقِ

The end of the Path consists of total absorption
in the direct witnessing of the Owner, the Creator.

إِيَّاكَ أَنْ تَصْغَىٰ لِطَاعِنٍ فِيهَا

لِجَهْلِهِ بِعِلْمِهَا وَفَضْلِهَا

Beware of listening to someone who might deny it
through his ignorance of its knowledge and excellence.

فَسَهِّلَنْ يَا رَبِّ لِلاِخْوَانِ

سُلُوكَهَا فَضْلًا بِلَا تَوَانِ

O Lord! Out of Your bounty
make its journey easy for the brotherhood without flagging.

قَدِ انْتَهَتْ خَوَارِقُ الطَّرِيقِ

لِمَنْ مَشَىٰ فِيهَا عَلَى التَّحْقِيقِ

This ends the Miracles of the Way
for the one who walks it gaining realisation.

فَارْحَمْ مُفِيدَهَا وَجَامِعًا لَهَا

وَمَنْ تَصَدَّىٰ مَعَنَا لِنَشْرِهَا

So have mercy on the one who related it, the one who collected it,
and whoever helps us to spread it.

نَاظِمُهَا مُحَمَّدُ ابْنُ الْحَبِيبْ

يَطْلُبُ لِلأُمَّةِ فَتْحًا فِي الْقَرِيبْ

The one who set it to verse, Muhammad ibn al-Habib,
asks Allah for an opening for the community soon,

وَنُصْرَةً لِظِلِّنَا الْمَحْبُوبْ

تُظْفِرُهُ بِجَمِيعِ الْمَرْغُوبْ

and for a victory for our beloved shelter
which will give him all his desires.

ثُمَّ صَلاَةُ اللهِ تَتْرَىٰ أَبَدًا

عَلَىٰ مُحَمَّدٍ وَمَنْ بِهِ اقْتَدَىٰ

May the blessings of Allah fall one after another eternally
on Muhammad and whoever copies him,

كَذَٰلِكَ الآلِ مَعَ الصِّحَابْ

اَلسَّالِكِينَ سُبُلَ الصَّوَابْ ۞

And also on his family and Companions,
the Salikeen who trod the paths of right action.

Virtues of the Ism al-A'dham

وتليه دالية في
فضائل الاسم الاعظم

تَجَرَّدْ عَنِ الاَغْيَارِ تَحْظَىٰ بِقُرْبِهِ
وَتَرْقَىٰ مَرَاقِي الْقَوْمِ فِي كُلِّ مَشْهَدِ

Free yourself from all that is other and you will attain His nearness,
and you will rise to the ranks of the People of every assembly.

وَعَمِّرْ بِذِكْرِ اللهِ أَنْفَاسَكَ الَّتِي
تُحَاسَبُ عنها يوْمَ حَشْرٍ ومَوْعِدِ

Fill your every breath with dhikr of Allah, because each breath
has to be accounted for on the Day of Gathering and promise.

وَعَظِّمْ جَمِيعَ الْكَوْنِ مِنْ حَيْثُ إِنَّهُ
تَكَوَّنَ مِنْ نُورِ النَّبِيِّ مُحَمَّدِ

Exalt all phenomena because they are formed
from the light of the Prophet Muhammad.

وَلَاحِظْهُ أَنْوَارًا لِأَسْمَاءِ رَبِّنَا

وَغِبْ عَنْ كَثَافَةٍ وَعَنْ قَوْلِ مُلْحِدِ

Regard them as lights from the Names of our Lord
and withdraw from being unresponsive and speaking from opinion.

وَأَحْبِبْ بِحُبِّ اللهِ وَابْغَضْ بِبَغْضِهِ

فَذَاكَ مِنَ التَّشْرِيعِ فَاحْفَظْهُ سَيِّدِي

Love with the love of Allah and hate with His hate.
This is the Shari'a so guard it, my friend!

وَكُنْ بَرْزَخَ الْبَحْرَيْنِ حَقٍّ وَشِرْعَةٍ

تَحُزْ رُتْبَةَ التَّعْرِيفِ فِي كُلِّ مَقْعَدِ

Be an isthmus between the two seas – the Haqiqa and the Shari'a,
and you will attain the rank of recognition in every assembly.

وَدُلَّ عِبَادَ اللهِ بِاللهِ مُعْلِنًا

بِتَحْسِينِ طُرْقِ اللهِ فِي كُلِّ مَسْجِدِ

In every mosque, guide the slaves of Allah by Allah
openly, by showing the beauty of the paths of Allah.

وَإِنْ شِئْتَ إِسْرَاعًا لِحَضْرَةِ رَبِّنَا

فَحَسِّنْ بِخَلْقِ اللهِ ظَنًّا وَمَجِّدِ

And if you wish to go swiftly into the presence of our Lord,
then have a good opinion of Allah's creation and praise Him.

وَوَاظِبْ عَلَى الِاسْمِ الْعَظِيمِ الْمُعَظَّمِ

بِحُسْنِ سَرِيرَةٍ وَصِدْقٍ وَمَقْصِدِ

Persevere with the sublime Ism al-'Adhim
in your secret, with sincerity and concentration.

وَشَاهِدْ جَمَالَ الذَّاتِ فِي كُلِّ مَظْهَرٍ

فَلَوْ لَا هَا لَمْ يَثْبُتْ وُجُودٌ لِمُوجَدِ

Witness the beauty of the Essence in every manifestation. Were it not for it –
the existence of the Existent would not have been established.

وَكُلُّ صِفَاتِ النَّفْسِ تَفْنَىٰ بِذِكْرِهِ

وَيَبْقَىٰ نَعِيمُ الْقَلْبِ أَحْلَىٰ مِنَ الشُّهْدِ

All the attributes of the self have fana' by His dhikr,
and the bliss of the heart remains, sweeter than honey.

وَكُلُّ تَحَلٍّ بِالْمَقَامَاتِ نَاشِئٌ

عَنِ الذِّكْرِ بِالِاسْمِ الْعَظِيمِ مَعَ الْجِدِّ

Every station is acquired through the dhikr
of the Ism al-'Adhim done with gravity.

فَمِنْهُ يَكُونُ الْفَتْحُ لِكُلِّ سَالِكٍ

وَمِنْهُ يَكُونُ الْفَيْضُ لِكُلِّ مُرْشِدِ

From it comes the Opening for every Salik,
and from it comes the overflowing for every Murshid.

وَعَنْهُ تَكُونُ حَالَةُ السُّكْرِ وَالْفَنَا

وَعَنْهُ تَكُونُ حَالَةُ الصَّحْوِ وَالْوَجْد

From it come the States of intoxication and fana',
and from it, too, the States of sobriety and ecstasy.

وَمَا نَالَ عِزًّا غَيْرُ مُنْفَرِدٍ بِهِ

تَحَلَّى بِمَا يُرْضِيهِ مَعْ كَثْرَةِ الْحَمْد

High rank is only given to the one isolated with Him,
who takes on what pleases Him along with much praise.

فَمَا زَالَ يَرْقَى فِي مَهَامَةِ ذَاتِهِ

وَيَفْنَى فَنَاءً لَيْسَ فِيهِ سِوَى الْفَقْد

Thus he will rise, crossing the deserts of His Essence, until
his fana' enters a fana' that has nothing in it but loss.

فَإِنْ رُدَّ لِلْآثَارِ جَاءَ بِحُلَّةٍ

تُنَادِي عَلَيْهِ بِالْوِلَايَةِ وَالْمَجْد

If he returns to the traces of existence, he brings
a Robe of Honour which proclaims his Wilaya and glory.

فَكُنْ خَادِمًا عَبْدًا لِمَنْ هٰذَا وَصْفُهُ

وَوَفِّ بِعَهْدِ اللهِ يَاتِكَ بِالْوَعْد

So be a servant and slave to the one whose description this is, and fulfil
the contract of Allah, and He will give you what He has promised.

وَأَعْظَمُ خَلْقِ اللهِ فِي ذَاكَ رُسْلُهُ

وَأَكْمَلُهُمْ فِيهِ النَّبِيُّ مُحَمَّدٌ

The greatest of Allah's creation in this matter are His Messengers,
and the most perfect of them in it is the Prophet Muhammad.

فَظَاهِرُهُ نُورٌ وَبَاطِنُهُ سِرُّ

اتُهُ لَيْسَتْ تُحَصَّلُ بِالْعَدّ

His outward is a light and his inward is a secret.
His perfections are beyond numbering.

عَلَيْهِ صَلَاةُ اللهِ وَالْآلِ وَالصَّحْبِ

وَدَارِكَا بِالْأَلْطَافِ مِنْ غَيْرِ مَا حَدّ ۞

May the blessings of Allah be upon him and his family and
Companions, and give us limitless and uninterrupted kindness.

121

Praise

وتليه رائية

الحمد

لَكَ الْحَمْدُ يَا ذَا الْحِلْمِ وَالْعَفْوِ وَالسِّتْرِ

وَحَمْدِيَ مِن نُّعْمَاكَ يَا وَاسِعَ الْبَرِّ

Praise is due to You the Possessor of forbearance,
forgiveness and veiling of our actions.
My praise is one of Your greatest blessings, O Abundant Goodness.

لَكَ الْحَمْدُ عَدَّ الْقَطْرِ وَالرَّمْلِ وَالْحَصَىٰ

وَعَدَّ نَبَاتِ الْأَرْضِ وَالْحُوتِ فِي الْبَحْرِ

Praise is due to You in number as great as the drops of rain,
grains of sand, pebbles, plants of the earth and fish in the sea.

لَكَ الْحَمْدُ عَدَّ النَّمْلِ وَالْجِنِّ وَالْاِنْسِ

وَمِلْءَ السَّمَا وَالْعَرْشِ وَالْكَوْكَبِ الدُّرِّ

Praise is due to You in number as great as the ants, jinn and men,
in quantity as great as the sky, the Throne and the pearly stars.

122

وَمِلْءَ الْفَضَا وَاللَّوْجِ وَالْكُرْسِي وَالثَّرَىٰ

وَعَدَّ جَمِيعِ الْكَائِنَاتِ إِلَى الْحَشْرِ

In quantity as great as space itself, the Tablet of Forms, the Footstool,
the moist earth, and the number of all living things on the Day of Gathering.

لَكَ الْحَمْدُ يَا رَبِّي كَمَا أَنْتَ أَهْلُهُ

فَإِنِّي لَا أُحْصِي الثَّنَاءَ مَدَى الدَّهْرِ

Praise is due to You, O my Lord, as much You deserve,
for I cannot praise You fittingly to the full extent of time.

لَكَ الْحَمْدُ يَا مُعْطِي الْمَوَاهِبِ بِالْفَضْلِ

وَمَانِحَ أَهْلِ اللهِ بِالْفَتْحِ وَالنَّصْرِ

Praise is due to You, O endless Giver of gifts,
the One Who grants opening and triumph to the people of Allah.

لَكَ الْحَمْدُ بِالْأَنْفَاسِ وَالْجِسْمِ وَالْقَلْبِ

تَفَضَّلْ عَلَىٰ عَبْدٍ تَحَيَّرَ فِي الْأَمْرِ

Praise is due to You with every breath, with the body and the heart.
Look kindly on a slave who is perplexed by affairs.

فَإِنِّي وَإِنْ كَانَتْ ذُنُوبِي تَعُوقُنِي

فَلِي فِيكَ حُسْنُ الظَّنِّ يَجْبِرُ لِي كَسْرِي

If my wrong actions weigh me down,
I still have a good opinion of You that mends my broken spirit.

فَمُنَّ عَلَيْنَا يَا غَفُورُ بِتَوْبَةٍ
تَجُبُّ الَّذِي قَدْ كَانَ فِي سَالِفِ الْعُمْرِ

O Forgiving! Give us tawba that will undo
what happened in our early years.

وَزِدْنَا مِنَ النَّعْمَاءِ وَالنُّورِ وَالْكَشْفِ
وَمَكِّنَّا فِي الْإِرْشَادِ بِالْإِذْنِ وَالسِّرِّ

Increase us in blessing, light and unveiling,
and strengthen us in guidance, with Idhn and the Secret.

وَأَيِّدْنَا فِي أَقْوَالِنَا وَفِعَالِنَا
وَيَسِّرْ لَنَا الْأَرْزَاقَ مِنْ حَيْثُ لَا نَدْرِي

Support us in our words and deeds,
and make our provision easy for us – from where we know not.

فَهَا نَحْنُ فِي بَابِ التَّفَضُّلِ وَاقِفٌ
وَمُنْتَظِرٌ عَطْفَ الْحَبِيبِ بِلَا عُسْرِ

Here we are standing at the door of favour,
waiting without hardship for the kindness of the Beloved.

فَأَنْعِمْ عَلَيْنَا يَا مُجِيبُ بِسُرْعَةٍ
فَإِنَّكَ أَهْلُ الْجُودِ وَالْمَنِّ وَالْخَيْرِ

Swiftly send us Your favour, O Answerer, for You are
the Possessor of generosity, liberality and goodness.

فَفَضْلُكَ مَوْجُودٌ بِغَيْرِ وُجُودِنَا

وَجُودُكَ مَسْدُولٌ عَلَيْنَا بِلَا نُكْرِ

Your bounty exists without our existence,
and undeniably it is Your Generosity that pours down on us.

فَوَفِّقْنَا لِلشُّكْرِ الَّذِي هُوَ لَازِمٌ

عَلَيْنَا وَيَسْتَدْعِي الْمَزِيدَ بِلَا خُسْرِ

Give us success in the thankfulness which is our duty
and which itself calls for increase from You without loss to us.

وَأَخْرِجْنَا مِنْ سِجْنِ الْجُسُومِ وَرَقِّنَا

لِحَضْرَةِ أَرْوَاحٍ ثَوَابًا عَلَى الشُّكْرِ

Free us from the prison of our bodies and raise us
up to the presence of the spirits as a reward for our gratitude.

وَأَشْهِدْنَا مَعْنَى الذَّاتِ فِي كُلِّ مَظْهَرٍ

لِيَقْوَىٰ شُهُودِي فِي الشَّدَائِدِ وَالْيُسْرِ

Let us see the meaning of the Essence in every manifestation
in order to strengthen our witnessing both in times of ease and trouble.

وَأَفْنِنَا عَنَّا وَابْقِنَا بِكَ دَائِمًا

لِنَلْحَقَ أَهْلَ الْإِرْثِ مِنْ حَضْرَةِ السِّرِّ

Annihilate us from ourselves and give us going-on in You always,
so that we may join the people who have inherited the presence of the secret.

فَأَمْرُكَ لِلَاشْيَاءِ فِي قَوْلِ كُنْ تَكُنْ

فَكَوِّنْ لَنَا الاَشْيَاءَ عَزْمًا بِلَا مَكْرِ

Your command to things is in the word 'Be, and it is.'
So shape things for us with firm intention and without deception.

وَصَلِّ بِأَنْوَاعِ الْكَمَالَاتِ كُلِّهَا

عَلَىٰ أَحْمَدَ الْهَادِي إِلَىٰ حَضْرَةِ الطُّهْرِ

Bless Ahmad, the guide to the Presence of purity,
with all the forms of perfection.

وَءَالِهِ وَالصَّحْبِ الْكِرَامِ وَمَنْ دَعَا

لِنَاظِمِ هَـٰذَا النَّظْمِ بِالشَّرْحِ فِي الْقَبْرِ

And his family and noble Companions and whoever prays
for expansion of the grave for the composer of these verses.

وَيَا رَبِّ بِالْهَادِي الرَّؤُوفِ مُحَمَّدٍ

أَنِلْنَا عُلُومًا تَنْفَعُنَا يَوْمَ النَّشْرِ

And O Lord! Through the compassionate guide, Muhammad,
grant us knowledges that will benefit us on the Day of Rising.

وَقَوِّنَا بِالاَنْوَارِ فِي كُلِّ لَحْظَةٍ

وَثَبِّتْنَا عِنْدَ الْخَتْمِ وَالنَّزْعِ وَالْقَبْرِ ۞

Strengthen us with lights at every instant, and make us
firm at the sealing, the agony of death, and the grave.

Stimulation of Desire for
the Act of Dhikr

وتليه رائية
الترغيب في الذكر

أَيَا مَنْ يُرِدْ قُرْبًا مِنَ اللهِ عَنْ فَوْرِ
عَلَيْكَ بِذِكْرِ اللهِ فِي السِّرِّ وَالْجَهْرِ

O you who desire nearness to Allah immediately
– you must perform dhikr of Allah openly and secretly.

وَعَمِّرْ بِهِ الأَوْقَاتَ تَسْمُو بِسُرْعَةٍ
إِلَىٰ ذِرْوَةِ الْعِرْفَانِ مَعْ خَالِصِ الْفِكْرِ

Fill the moments with it and you will swiftly
ascend to the pinnacle of gnosis with pure reflection.

لِتَصْقِيلِ مِرْءَا الْقَلْبِ يَنْكَشِفُ الْغِطَا
وَتَبْدُو لَهُ الأَنْوَارُ مِنْ خَالِصِ الذِّكْرِ

Through polishing the mirror of the heart, the veil is removed,
and lights appear to it from the purity of the dhikr.

بِذِكْرٍ إِلَهِ الْعَرْشِ تَزْهَدُ فِي الْوَرَى
وَتَفْنَى عَنِ النَّفْسِ الْمُعَطِّلَةِ السَّيْرِ

By dhikr of the God of the Throne you will come to do without people,
and you will be annihilated from the self, which delays you on the journey.

وَتَضْحَى جَلِيسَ اللهِ مِنْ غَيْرِ كُلْفَةٍ
وَتَسْلَمُ مِنْ شَكٍّ وَشِرْكٍ وَمِنْ غَيْرٍ

You will become one who sits with Allah, without ceremony,
and you will be safe from doubt, shirk and otherness.

وَتَرْحَلُ عَنْ كَوْنٍ إِلَى حَضْرَةِ الصَّفَا
وَتَشْهَدُ فِعْلَ اللهِ فِي الْخَلْقِ وَالْأَمْرِ

You will journey from the cosmos to the presence of Purity,
and you will witness the act of Allah in the creation and in affairs.

وَتَرْقَى إِلَى الْأَسْمَاءِ تُسْقَى بِنُورِهَا
فَتَبْدُو لَكَ الْأَوْصَافُ مِنْ غَيْرِ مَا سِتْرٍ

You will rise to the Names and drink of their light,
and the Attributes will appear to you without a veil.

وَيَظْهَرُ مَعْنَى الذَّاتِ مِنْ كَامِلِ الْفَنَا
فَتَبْقَى غَنِيًّا بِالْإِلَهِ مَدَى الْعُمْرِ

The meaning of the Essence will emerge from the perfection of Fana',
and you will go on, rich with Allah for the rest of your life.

فَإِنْ عَبِقَتْ فِي الْغَرْبِ أَنْفَاسُ ذِكْرِهِ

وَفِي الشَّرْقِ مَعْلُولٌ تَعَافَىٰ مِنَ الضُّرِّ

If the breath of His dhikr were to fill the west and there was a sick man
in the east, that man would be cured of his affliction.

عَلَيْهِ مَدَارُ الدِّينِ فِي كُلِّ قُرْبَةٍ

وَلَا سِيَمَا ذِكْرُ الْجَلَالَةِ مِنْ حُرِّ

In every drawing near, it is the pivot of the Deen,
especially the dhikr of Majesty by one who is free.

فَمَا مِنْ وَلِيٍّ إِلَّا هَامَ بِذِكْرِهِ

عَلَىٰ عَدَدِ الْأَنْفَاسِ بِالرُّوحِ وَالسِّرِّ

There is no Wali who is not infatuated with His dhikr,
with his ruh and his secret, in every breath.

فَقَدْ كَانَ ذَاكِرًا وَأَصْبَحَ مَذْكُورًا

يَتِيهُ عَلَى الْأَكْوَانِ مِنْ غَيْرِ مَا فَخْرِ

He was a rememberer and he became remembered,
and this gave him superiority over creatures, without boasting.

وَمَا الْفَخْرُ إِلَّا بِالْعُبُودِيَّةِ الَّتِي

تَخَلَّصَتْ مِنْ حَوْلٍ وَقُوًىٰ وَمِنْ مَكْرِ

There is no boasting except in slavedom,
freed from strength, power and self-deception.

129

نَتَائِجُ ذِكْرِ اللهِ لَيْسَ لَهَا حَصْرُ

فَوَاظِبْ أَخِي وَلَوْ عَشِيًّا وَبِالْفَجْرِ

The results of dhikr of Allah are without limit,
so, my brother, persevere even if only in the evening and at Fajr.

لَقَدْ وَرَدَ الْإِكْثَارُ مِنْهُ بِلَا حَدِّ

تَصَفَّحْ كِتَابَ اللهِ مَعَ سُنَّةٍ تَدْرِي

Doing a lot of it without limit is transmitted;
study the Book of Allah along with the Sunna and you will understand.

وَقَدْ وَعَدَ الْجَلِيلُ بِذِكْرٍ مَنْ غَدَا

لَهُ ذَاكِرًا يَا فَوْزَ مَنْ خُصَّ بِالذِّكْرِ

The Glorious has promised to remember whoever remembers Him –
Oh the victory of someone who is singled out by dhikr!

وَمَنْ يَعْشُ عَنْ ذِكْرِ الْإِلَهِ يَكُنْ لَهُ

قَرِينٌ مِنَ الشَّيْطَانِ يَفْتِنُ عَنْ سَيْرِ

Whoever turns away from dhikr of God has a companion
allotted to him from Shaytan to tempt him from the journey.

فَلَا يَطْمَئِنُّ الْقَلْبُ إِلَّا بِذِكْرِهِ

فَيَسْكُنَ عَنْ خَوْفِ الْخَلِيقَةِ وَالْفَقْرِ

The heart is only made tranquil by His dhikr,
and it is calmed from fear of creation and poverty.

وَلَا تُبْسَطُ الْأَرْزَاقُ إِلَّا لِمَنْ غَدَا

يُرَدِّدهُ حَتَّى يَغِيبَ فِي الْوِتْرِ

Provision is only assured for the one who goes forth in the morning
repeating it until he absents himself in the One.

وَهَذَا رَسُولُ اللهِ يَذْكُرُ دَائِمًا

عَلَى كُلِّ أَحْيَانٍ يَشْرَعُ لِلْغَيْرِ

The Messenger of Allah did dhikr constantly at all times,
laying down the road for others.

وَقَالَ اذْكُرُوا حَتَّى يَقُولُونَ إِنَّهُ

يُرَائِي بِذِكْرِ اللهِ حِرْصًا عَلَى الْخَيْرِ

He said, 'Do dhikr until they say, "He is showing off
with dhikr of Allah"' out of eagerness for the blessing.

عَلَيْكَ بِهِ فَالْقَوْمُ قَدْ سَكِرُوا بِهِ

وَأَفْنَوْا فِيهِ الْأَرْوَاحَ يَالَهُ مِنْ ذُخْرٍ

You must do it, for the People have become intoxicated by it,
and they have annihilated their spirits in it – what a treasure for them!

فَكُلُّ مَقَامَاتِ الرِّجَالِ قَدِ انْطَوَتْ

فِي حُبِّ وَذِكْرِ اللهِ بِالْفَمِ وَالصَّدْرِ

All the stations of the Men are contained
in love and dhikr of Allah with mouth and heart.

وَلَا تَكْتَفِي بِالْوَارِدَاتِ عَنِ الْوِرْدِ

وَلَا تَطْلُبَنْ إِلَّا رِضَاهُ مَعَ السِّتْرِ

Do not be satisfied with lights that descend on the heart from the Wird;
only ask for His approval along with veiling of wrong actions.

فَيَا رَبِّ وَفِّقْنَا لِصِدْقِ تَوَجُّهٍ

بِجَاهِ الَّذِي قَدْ جَاءَ بِالْفَتْحِ وَالنَّصْرِ

So, O Lord, give us success in sincere turning to you,
by the rank of the one who brought an opening and a triumph.

مُحَمَّدٌ أَصْلُ الْمَوْجُودَاتِ وَسِرُّهَا

وَخَاتِمُ رُسْلِ اللهِ وَالْاَنْبِيَا الْغُرِّ

Muhammad is the source and secret of existent beings,
and the seal of the Messengers of Allah and the glorious Prophets.

عَلَيْهِ صَلَاةُ اللهِ مَا هَامَ ذَاكِرٌ

بِذِكْرِ مَوْلَاهُ فِي الشَّدَائِدِ وَالْيُسْرِ

May the blessings of Allah be upon him as long as there is someone
in love with the remembrance of his Lord in times of trial and ease –

وَءَالِهِ وَالْاَصْحَابِ مَعْ كُلِّ مُقْتَفٍ

مُتَابَعَةَ الْمُخْتَارِ فِي النَّهْيِ وَالْاَمْرِ ۞

– and on his family and Companions and every follower
who follows the Chosen One in prohibition and command.

Reflection

وتليه رائية

التفكر

تَفَكَّرْ جَمِيلَ الصُّنع فِي الْبَرِّ وَالْبَحْرِ

وَجُلْ فِي صِفَاتِ اللهِ فِي السِّرِّ وَالْجَهْرِ

Reflect upon the beauty of the way in which both the land and sea are made,
and contemplate the Attributes of Allah openly and secretly.

وَفِي النَّفْسِ وَالآفَاقِ أَعْظَمُ شَاهِدٍ

عَلَى كَمَالَاتِ اللهِ مِنْ غَيْرِ مَا حَصْرِ

The greatest evidence of the limitless perfections of Allah
can be found both deep within the self and on the distant horizon.

فَلَوْ جُلْتَ فِي الاَجْسَامِ مَعْ حُسْنِ شَكْلِهَا

وَتَنْظِيمِهَا تَنْظِيمَ خَيْطٍ مِنَ الدُّرِّ

If you were to reflect on physical bodies and their marvellous forms
and how they are arranged with great precision, like a string of pearls;

وَجُلْتَ فِي أَسْرَارِ اللِّسَانِ وَنُطْقِه
وَتَعْبِيرِه عَمَّا تُكِنُّهُ فِي الصَّدْرِ

and if you were to reflect on the secrets of the tongue and its speech,
and how it articulates and conveys what you conceal in your breast;

وَجُلْتَ فِي أَسْرَارِ الْجَوَارِحِ كُلِّهَا
وَتَسْخِيرِهَا لِلْقَلْبِ مِنْ غَيْرِ مَا عُسْرِ

and if you were to reflect on the secrets of all the limbs
and how easily they are subject to the heart's command;

وَجُلْتَ فِي تَقْلِيبِ الْقُلُوبِ لِطَاعَةٍ
وَفِي بَعْضِ أَحْيَانٍ لِمَعْصِيَةٍ تَسْرِي

and if you were to reflect on how the hearts are moved to obey Allah
and how sometimes they move to disobedience;

وَجُلْتَ فِي أَرْضٍ مَعَ تَنَوُّعِ نَبْتِهَا
وَكَثْرَةِ مَا فِيهَا مِنَ السَّهْلِ وَالْوَعْرِ

and if you were to reflect on the earth and the diversity of its plants
and the great varieties of plains and rugged mountains in it;

وَجُلْتَ فِي أَسْرَارِ الْبِحَارِ وَحُوتِهَا
وَكَثْرَةِ أَمْوَاجٍ لَهَا حَاجِزٌ قَهْرِ

and if you were to reflect on the secrets of the oceans and all their fish,
and their endless waves held back by an unconquerable barrier;

وَجُلْتَ فِي أَسْرَارِ الرِّيَاحِ وَجَلْبِهَا
لِغَيْمٍ وَسُحْبٍ قَدْ أَسَالَتْ مِنَ الْقَطْرِ

and if you were to reflect on the secrets of the many winds
and how they bring the mist, fog and clouds which release the rain;

وَجُلْتَ فِي أَسْرَارِ السَّمَـٰوَٰتِ كُلِّهَا
وَعَرْشٍ وَكُرْسِيٍّ وَرُوحٍ مِنَ الْأَمْرِ

and if you were to reflect on all the secrets of the heavens –
the Throne, the Footstool and the spirit which is Allah's Affair –

عَقَدْتَ عَلَى التَّوْحِيدِ عَقْدَ مُصَمِّمٍ
وَحُلْتَ عَنِ الْأَوْهَامِ وَالشَّكِّ وَالْغَيْرِ

then you would accept the reality of Tawhid with all your being,
and you would turn away from illusions, uncertainty and otherness;

وَقُلْتَ إِلَهِي أَنْتَ سُؤْلِي وَمَطْلَبِي
وَحِصْنِي مِنَ الْأَسْوَاءِ وَالضَّيْمِ وَالْمَكْرِ

and you would say, 'My God, You are my desire, my goal
and my impregnable fortress against evil, injustice, and deceit.

وَأَنْتَ رَجَائِي فِي قَضَاءِ حَوَائِجِي
وَأَنْتَ الَّذِي تُنْجِي مِنَ السُّوءِ وَالشَّرِّ

'You are the One I hope will provide for all my needs,
and You are the One Who rescues us from all evil and wickedness.

وَأَنْتَ الرَّحِيمُ الْمُسْتَجِيبُ لِمَنْ دَعَاكَ

وَأَنْتَ الَّذِي تُغْنِي الْفَقِيرَ عَنِ الْفَقْرِ

'You are the Compassionate, the One Who answers all who call on You.
And You are the One Who frees the needy of their need.

إِلَيْكَ رَفَعْتُ يَا رَفِيعُ مَطَالِبِي

فَعَجِّلْ بِفَتْحٍ يَا إِلَهِي مَعَ السِّرِّ

'It is to You, O Exalted, that I have raised all my requests,
so swiftly bring me the Opening along with the Secret, O my God.'

بِجَاهِ الَّذِي يُرْجَىٰ يَوْمَ الْكَرْبِ وَالْعَنَا

وَيَوْمَ وُرُودِ النَّاسِ لِلْمَوْقِفِ الْحَشْرِ

By the rank of the one who is hoped for on the day of distress and grief,
and the day when people come to the Place of Gathering,

عَلَيْهِ صَلَاةُ اللهِ مَا جَالَ عَارِفٌ

فِي أَنْوَارِ ذَاتِهِ لَدَىٰ كُلِّ مَظْهَرِ

may Allah's blessings be upon him as long as there is a gnostic
who reflects on the lights of His Essence in every manifestation,

وَءَالِهِ وَالْاَصْحَابِ مَعَ كُلِّ تَابِعٍ

لِسُنَّتِهِ الْغَرَّاءِ فِي النَّهْيِ وَالْاَمْرِ ۞

and upon his family and Companions and everyone who follows
his excellent Sunna in prohibition and command.

Robe of Nearness

وتليه رائية

حلة التقريب

قَدْ كَسَانَا ذِكْرُ الْحَبِيبِ جَمَالًا
وَبَهَاءً وَرِفْعَةً وَسُرُورًا

Remembrance of the Beloved clothed us
in beauty, radiance, exaltation and joy.

وَخَلَعْنَا الْعِذَارَ عِنْدَ التَّدَانِي
وَجَهَرْنَا بِمَنْ نُحِبُّ افْتِخَارَا

In drawing near we cast aside every restraint
and openly proclaimed the One we love, glorying in Him.

وَسَقَانَا الْحَبِيبُ شَرْبَةَ حُبٍّ
قَدْ أَزَالَتْ سِوَى الْحَبِيبِ اضْطِرَارَا

The Beloved gave us a draught of pure love to drink
which forced all but the Beloved to disappear.

وَشَهِدْنَا الاَكْوَانَ مَحْضَ هَبَاءٍ
وَرَأَيْنَا الاَنْوَارَ تَبْدُو جِهَارَا

We witnessed beings as pure specks of dust;
we saw the lights appear openly.

وَرَجَعْنَا لِلْخَلْقِ بَعْدَ انْمِحَاقٍ
وَفَنَاءٍ فِي خَمْرَةٍ تُعْطِي نُورَا

After having been obliterated and annihilated
in a light-giving wine, we returned to creation.

فَبِفَضْلٍ مِنَ الالَهِ بَقِينَا
وَكَتَمْنَا الَّذِي نُحِبُّ اصْطِبَارَا

By a pure gift from God we were given Baqa,
and so, with patience, we concealed the One we love.

كَمْ نَظَرْنَا فِي سَالِكٍ فَتَرَقَّى١
لِمَقَامِ الَّذِينَ خَاضُوا الْبِحَارَا

How often have we looked on a wayfarer who has then risen
to the stations of those who have plunged into the seas!

وَشَفَيْنَا الْقُلُوبَ مِمَّا عَرَاهَا
بِلَطِيفِ الْعُلُومِ ذَوْقًا فَطَارَا

We have healed hearts of what had befallen them
through knowledges of subtle taste, and they have soared.

وَهَمَمْنَا بِالشَّيْءِ سِرًّا فَكَانَا

وَأَتَانَا الَّذِي نُحِبُّ اخْتِيَارَا

We concerned ourselves with something secretly, so that it came about,
and the One we have chosen to love has come to us.

وَسَمِعْنَا مِنْ حَضْرَةِ الْغَيْبِ سِرًّا

أَنْتَ مَحْبُوبٌ عِنْدَنَا كُنْ شَكُورَا

We heard a secret from the presence of the Unseen
'In Our sight you are beloved so be grateful.'

وَأُذِنَّا بِسَقْيِ مَنْ جَاءَ شَوْقًا

لِلِقَانَا وَلَمْ يَكُنْ ذَا اخْتِبَارَا

We were granted Idhn to quench the thirst of whoever comes longing
to meet us, and not just researching.

وَإِذَا كَانَتِ الْمَوَاهِبُ فَضْلًا

فَتَعَرَّضْ لَهَا وَكُنْ ذَا افْتِقَارَا

If gifts are abundant,
expose yourself to them, and be a needy person.

وَتَذَلَّلْ لِأَهْلِهَا تُسْقَىٰ مِنْهُم

وَتَقَرَّبْ لَهُمْ وَلَا تَخْشَ عَارَا

Humble yourselves to their people – they will satisfy your thirst.
Draw near to them and have no fear of disgrace.

وَتَجَرَّدْ مِنْ كُلِّ عِلْمٍ وفَهْمٍ

لِتَنَالَ الَّذِي نَالُوهُ الْكِبَارَا

Strip yourselves of all knowledge and understanding
so that you may obtain what the great have obtained.

وَابْذُلِ النَّفْسَ يَا مُحِبَّ الْوِصَالِ

وَاتَّبِعِ الشَّيْخَ فِي الَّذِي قَدْ أَشَارَا

Freely offer up your self, you who desire arrival,
and follow the Shaykh in whatever he indicates.

وَاشْهَدِ الْحَقَّ فِيهِ ذَاتًا وَقَلْبًا

وَافْنَ فِيهِ تَكُنْ بِهِ ذَا انْتِصَارَا

Witness the truth in him, in both your essence and your heart,
annihilate yourself in him; by him you will gain victory.

فَهْوَ نُورُ الرَّسُولِ مِنْ كُلِّ وَجْهٍ

وَهْوَ طِبُّ الْقُلُوبِ سِرًّا وَجَهْرَا

He is the light of the Messenger in every aspect,
and the medicine of hearts, both openly and secretly.

فَالْحَظْنْهُ وَعَظِّمَنْهُ كَثِيرَا

وَاذْهَبَنْ عِنْدَهُ وَكُنْ ذَا انْكِسَارَا

Pay attention to him and show him great esteem.
Go into his presence in a broken condition.

140

وَصَلَاةٌ عَلَى النَّبِيِّ وَءَالٍ

وَصِحَابٍ وَمَنْ لَهُ قَدْ أَشَارَا

Blessings be upon the Prophet and all his family
and Companions and all who direct people to him,

وَسَلَامٌ بِكُلِّ مِسْكٍ وَطِيبٍ

وَجَمَالٍ وَرِفْعَةٍ لَا تُجَارَا ۞

and peace, fragrant with musk and every scent,
beauty and unrivalled sublimity.

Qasida Written Before the Prophet

وتليها اللامية التي انشأها تجاه
النبي صلى الله عليه وسلم

نَحْنُ فِي رَوْضَةِ الرَّسُولِ حُضُورُ
طَالِبِينَ الرِّضَىٰ وَحُسْنَ قَبُولِ

We are present in the Rawda of the Messenger,
hoping for acceptance and welcome.

جِئْنَا يَا خَيْرَ مَنْ إِلَيْهِ الْمَلَاذُ
بِانْكِسَارٍ وَذِلَّةٍ وَذُهُولِ

We have come, O best of refuges! –
broken, humbled and confused.

فَاسْأَلِ اللهَ فِينَا كُلَّ عِنَايَهْ
لِنَنَالَ الْمُنَىٰ فِي وَقْتِ الْحُلُولِ

Ask Allah to show every concern for us,
so that our hopes will be fulfilled at the time debts fall due.

142

لَكَ قَدْرٌ عَظِيمٌ لَيْسَ يُضَاهَى
وَرِسَالَهْ تَفُوقُ كُلَّ رَسُولِ

You have a vast power which is beyond compare,
and a message greater than every Messenger's.

أَنْتَ بَابُ الْالَهِ فِي كُلِّ خَيْرٍ
مَنْ أَتَى فَازَ بِالرِّضَى وَالْوُصُولِ

You are the door to God in every good thing,
whoever comes to you gains acceptance and union.

كُلُّ سِرٍّ فِي الْانْبِيَا قَدْ أَتَاهُمْ
مِنْ عَلَاكُمْ مُؤَيَّدًا بِنَقُولِ

Every secret which came to the Prophets
is from your sublimity, confirmed through transmission.

قَدْ تَشَفَّعْتُ فِي أُمُورِي إِلَاهِي
بِالنَّبِيِّ الْمُشَفَّعِ الْمَقْبُولِ

I have looked to the Prophet to intercede with God in my affair,
for he is the accepted intercessor.

كُلُّ مَنْ حَطَّ رَحْلَهُ بِكَرِيمٍ
نَالَ أَقْصَى الْمُنَى وَكُلَّ السُّولِ

All of those whose journey ends at the house of a generous host,
get everything they ask for, even their most extreme wish.

قَدْ شَكَرْنَا الالَهَ فِي كُلِّ وَقْتٍ
حَيْثُ مَنَّ بِزَوْرَةٍ لِرَسُولِ

We have given thanks to God for every time that He
has given us the gift of a visit to the Messenger –

وَكَذَاكَ لِكُلِّ مَنْ فِي بَقِيعٍ
مِنْ صِحَابٍ كَذَاكَ نَسْلُ الْبَتُولِ

and a visit to the Companions
and the offspring of Fatimah Batul in Baqi';

وَكَذَاكَ لِكُلِّ زَوْجٍ وَبِنْتٍ
وَابْنِ مُنْجِي الانَامِ يَوْمَ الْحُلُولِ

and a visit to every wife, daughter and son of the
deliverer of mankind on the day debts fall due;

وَكَذَاكَ لِكُلِّ مَنْ فِي أُحُدٍ
مِنْ شَهِيدٍ كَذَاكَ عَمُّ الرَّسُولِ

and a visit to every Shahid in Uhud,
and the uncle of the Messenger.

قَدْ طَلَبْنَا بِهِمْ تَمَامَ السَّلَامَهْ
فِي مَسِيرٍ لِأَرْضِنَا وَالدُّخُولِ

We have sought, by them, perfect safety for us on our
homeward journey and on our arrival.

وَطَلَبْنَا النَّجَاةَ فِي يَوْمِ حَشْرٍ
وَسَلَامًا مِنْ كُلِّ فَظٍّ جَهُولِ

We have sought rescue on the Day of Gathering
and safety from every ignorant, coarse person.

رَبِّ صَلِّ عَلَى النَّبِيِّ وَءَالٍ
وَصِحَابٍ وَتَابِعٍ بِشُمُولِ ۞

Our Lord, bless the Prophet and his family
and Companions and all the followers.

Withdrawal into the Perception of the Essence

وتليه رائية
الغيبة في شهود الذات

قَدْ بَدَا وَجْهُ الْحَبِيبِ
لَاحَ فِي وَقْتِ السَّحَرْ

The Face of the Beloved appeared
and shone in the pre-dawn.

نُورُهُ قَدْ عَمَّ قَلْبِي
فَسَجَدْتُ بِانْكِسَـارْ

His light pervaded my heart,
so I prostrated myself in awe.

قَالَ لِي ارْفَعْ وَاسْأَلَنِّي
فَلَكُمْ كُلُّ وَطَـرْ

He said to me, 'Rise! – ask of Me!
You will have whatever you desire.'

قُلْتُ أَنْتَ أَنْتَ حَسْبِي
لَيْسَ لِي عَنْكَ اصْطِبَارْ

I replied, 'You. You are enough for me!
Away from You I cannot live!'

قَالَ عَبْدِي لَكَ بُشْرَىٰ
فَتَنَعَّمْ بِالنَّظَرْ

He said, 'My slave, there is good news for you,
so enjoy the vision.

أَنْتَ كَنْزٌ لِعِبَادِي
أَنْتَ ذِكْرَىٰ لِلْبَشَرْ

'You are a treasure for My slaves
and you are a reminder for mankind.

كُلُّ حُسْنٍ وَجَمَالٍ
فِي الْوَرَىٰ مِنِّي انْتَشَرْ

'Every good and every beauty in mankind
has spread from Me.

بَطَنَتْ أَوْصَافُ ذَاتِي
وَتَجَلَّتْ فِي الْأَثَرْ

'The Attributes of My Essence were hidden,
and they manifested themselves in creation.

إِنَّمَا الْكَوْنُ مَعَانٍ
قَـائِمَاتٌ بِالصُّوَرْ

'Created beings are only meanings
projected in forms.

كُلُّ مَنْ يُدْرِكُ هٰذَا
كَانَ مِنْ أَهْلِ الْعِبَـرْ

'All who grasp this
are among the people of discrimination.

لَمْ يَذُقْ لَذَّةَ عَيْشٍ
اَلَّذِي عَنَّا انْحَصَـرْ

'The one who is prevented from reaching Us
has not tasted the sweetness of life.'

رَبَّنَا صَلِّ عَلَىٰ مَنْ
نُورُهُ عَمَّ الْبَشَرْ

O Lord, bless the one whose light has spread
through all mankind,

وَءَالٍ مَعَ صِحَابٍ
مَا لَاحَ نُورُ الْقَمَرْ ۞

and the family and Companions
as long as the light of the moon shines.

The Qualities of Muhammad

وتليه لامية
الشمائل

مُحَمَّدٌ مَنْشَؤُ الاَنْوَارِ وَالظِّلَلِ
وَأَصْلُ تَكْوِينِهَا مِنْ حَضْرَةِ الاَزَلِ

Muhammad is the fountain-head of lights and darkness and
the source of their emergence from the presence of before-time.

فَنُورُهُ أَوَّلُ الاَنْوَارِ لَمَّا قَضَىٰ
إِظْهَارَ أَسْمَائِهِ فِي الْعَالَمِ الاَوَّلِ

His light was the first of lights when He determined
the manifestation of His Names in the first world.

مِنْهُ اكْتَسَتْ سَائِرُ الاَشْيَاءِ إِيجَادَهَا
وَمِنْهُ إِمْدَادُهَا مِنْ غَيِرِ مَا خَلَلِ

From him all things were clothed in their origination in existence,
and their continuance comes from him without interruption.

تَقَاطَرَ الْاَنْبِيَا وَالرُّسْلُ مِنْهُ كَمَا

تَقَاطَرَتْ سَائِرُ الْاَمْلَاكِ وَالْحُلَلِ

The Prophets and Messengers have come from him one by one,
as well as all the angels and all the creatures.

فَنِسْبَةُ الْخَتْمِ وَالْاَقْطَابِ مِنْ نُورِهِ

كَنُقْطَةٍ مِنْ بُحُورِ النُّورِ وَالْبَلَلِ

The relationship of the Seal and the Poles to his light
is that of a drop to oceans of light and refreshment.

وَالشَّمْسُ وَالْبَدْرُ وَالنُّجُومُ مِنْهُ بَدَتْ

كَالْعَرْشِ وَاللَّوْحِ وَالْكُرْسِيِّ وَالدُّوَلِ

The sun, moon and stars have appeared from him,
as have the Throne, Tablet, Footstool, and the dynasties.

فَشَاهِدِ النُّورَ قَدْ عَمَّ الْوُجُودَ وَلَا

تَكُنْ تَرَىٰ غَيْرَهُ تَصِلْ عَلَىٰ عَجَلِ

Witness the light which has spread through existence
and do not see other-than-it, and you will soon arrive.

لِاَنَّهُ الْمَظْهَرُ الْاَعْلَىٰ لِاَسْمَائِهِ

وَسِرُّ أَوْصَافِهِ مِنْ غَيْرِ مَا عِلَلِ

For he is the highest manifestation of Allah's Names
and the perfect unfaulted secret of His Attributes.

فَاللهُ إِخْتَارَهُ فِي عِلْمِهِ الْقَدِيمِ

لِلْخَلْقِ أَرْسَلَهُ طُرًّا وَلِلرُّسُلِ

Allah chose him in His timeless knowledge
and sent him to all of creation and to the other Messengers.

أَسْرَىٰ بِهِ اللهُ لَيْلًا بَعْدَ مَبْعَثِهِ

لِقَابِ قَوْسَيْنِ حَتَّىٰ فَازَ بِالأَمَلِ

After sending him as a Messenger, Allah conveyed him one night
to the distance of two bow-spans until he achieved his desire.

وَاسْتَبْشَرَ الْعَالَمُ الْعُلْوِيُّ لَمَّا رَقَىٰ

وَالْعَرْشُ قَدْ حَصَّلَ الأَمَانَ مِنْ وَجَلِ

The higher world rejoiced when he ascended,
and the Throne gave him security from fear.

وَاخْتَرَقَ الْحُجُبَ وَالأَنْوَارَ حَتَّىٰ دَنَا

وَنُودِيَ ادْنُ حَبِيبِي وَاسْكُنْ مِنْ خَجَلِ

He passed through the veils and lights until he drew near,
and he was summoned, 'Draw near, Beloved, and set aside your shyness.'

وَمَتِّعِ اللَّحْظَ فِي أَنْوَارِنَا وَاطْلُبَنْ

كُلَّ الَّذِي شِئْتَهُ تُعْطَ بِلَا مَلَلِ

'Rejoice in the sight of Our lights and demand all you want
and it will be given to you without delay.'

151

فَأُرْجِعَ الْمُصْطَفَىٰ بِكُلِّ مَكْرُمَةٍ
وَأَخْبَرَ النَّاسَ بِالاَقْصَا وَبِالسُّبُلِ

Then the Chosen One was returned with every noble quality
and he informed the people about al-Aqsa and the roads to it.

فَلُذْ بِهِ يَا أَخِي فِي كُلِّ مُعْضِلَةٍ
يَضْحَىٰ حَدِيثُكَ بَيْنَ النَّاسِ كَالْعَسَلِ

Take refuge with him in every dilemma, O my brother,
and your speech among the people will become like honey.

وَلَذِّذِ السَّمْعَ بِالاَخْلَاقِ وَالشِّيَمِ
وَاذْكُرْ شَمَائِلَهُ وَاحْذَرْ مِنَ الزَّلَلِ

Delight in hearing of his good character and qualities,
and evoke his virtues, and remain on guard against mistakes.

فَكَمْ خَوَارِقَ قَدْ جَاءَتْ عَلَىٰ يَدِهِ
فَأَعْجَزَتْ سَائِرَ الْحُسَّادِ وَالْمِلَلِ

How many miracles have come from his hand,
leaving the envious and all other religions powerless!

وَإِنَّ أَعْظَمَ خَارِقٍ لَهُ ظَهَرَا
هٰذَا الْكِتَابُ الَّذِي قَدْ جَاءَ بِالْعَمَلِ

The greatest of the miracles which were manifested for him
is this Book which brought us action.

فِي كُلِّ جَارِحَةٍ مِنْهُ فَوَائِدُ لَا

يُحْصِيهَا عَدٌّ وَلَا تُدْرِكُهَا بِالْمُقَلِ

In every act from it there are innumerable benefits,
which are not perceptible to the eyes.

وَقَدْ أَحَاطَ كِتَابُ اللهِ مِنْهَا بِمَا

يُبْرِئُ كُلَّ سَقِيمِ الْقَلْبِ مِنْ عِلَلِ

The Book of Allah contains some of these benefits
by which every one who is sick of heart is healed of his sickness.

وَلَيْسَ يَقْدُرُ قَدْرَهُ الْعَظِيمِ فَتًى

فَالْعَجْزُ عَنْ مَدْحِهِ مِنْ أَحْسَنِ السُّبُلِ

No hero is capable of attaining his mighty rank,
so the inability to praise him is the best of ways.

وَقَدْ تَشَبَّهْتُ فِي مَدْحِي وَجِئْتُ إِلَىٰ

رُحْمَاكَ مُسْتَشْفِعًا لِلَّهِ تَشْفَعُ لِي

I have copied you in my praise and I have come to your compassion
seeking intercession with Allah, so intercede on my behalf!

يَا أَعْظَمَ الْخَلْقِ عِنْدَ اللهِ مَنْزِلَةً

اِعْطِفْ عَلَيْنَا بِمَا نَرْجُوهُ يَا أَمَلِي

O greatest of creation with Allah in rank,
be kind to us with what we hope for, O my desire!

مَنْ يَحْتَمِي بِكَ يَضْحَى الْكَوْنُ يَخْدمه
لِأَجْلِ جَاهِكَ يَا مُدَّ كُلِّ وَلِي

By your rank, created beings serve whoever
seeks shelter with you, O Protector of every Wali.

بِكَ احْتَمَيْتُ فَلَا تَكِلْنِي يَا سَنَدِي
لِلنَّفْسِ وَالْجِنْسِ وَاجْبُرْنَا مِنَ الْخَلَلِ

O my support! I have sought shelter with you,
so do not leave me to my self and my humanness, but mend our faults.

وَلَيْسَ يَلْحَقُ عَبْدٌ أَنْتَ نَاصِرُه
فَأَنْتَ لِي عُمْدَةٌ فِي السَّهْلِ وَالْجَبَلِ

Nothing befalls the slave if you are his helper.
You are my staff on the level land and on the mountains.

وَقَدْ تَحَيَّرْتُ فِي أَمْرِي خُذْ بِيَدِي
فَلَا تَحَوَّلَ لِي عَنْ نُورِكَ الأَوَّلِ

I have become confused about myself, so take me by the hand.
For me there is no turning away from your first light.

صَلَّى عَلَيْكَ إِلَهُ الْعَرْشِ مَا ظَهَرَتْ
شَمْسُ الْحَقِيقَةِ بِالأَسْمَاءِ وَالْفِعَالِ

May the God of the Throne bless you as long
as the sun of the reality is manifested by the Names and the Acts.

154

كَذَٰلِكَ ءَالُكَ وَالِاصْحَابُ مَا نَبَتَتْ

عُشْبٌ وَمَا سَحَّتِ السَّمَاءُ مِنْ بِلَلِ

As well as your family and Companions as long as the grass grows
and the sky pours down abundant rain.

ثُمَّ الرِّضَىٰ عَنْ رِجَالِ اللهِ كُلِّهِمِ

مَا سَبَّحَ الْكَوْنُ مَنْ يُجَلُّ عَنْ مَثَلِ

Then I ask for Your good pleasure for all the Men of Allah
as long as beings glorify the One Who is above identification with forms.

وَابْسُطْ لِإِخْوَانِنَا الْخَيْرَاتِ أَجْمَعَهَا

دُنْيَا وَأُخْرَىٰ وَلَا تَكِلْنَا لِلْعَمَلِ

And unfold all blessings on our brothers, in this world and the next,
and do not leave us to our actions.

وَاغْفِرْ لِوَالِدِينَا الزَّلَّاتِ أَجْمَعَهَا

وَالْمُسْلِمِينَ بِفَضْلٍ مِنْكَ يَا أَزَلِي ۞

Forgive our parents all their mistakes, and the Muslims,
by an outpouring from You – O Before-endless-time!

Forgiveness

وتليها لامية
الاستغفار

أَسْتَغْفِرُ اللهَ إِنَّ اللهَ ذُو كَرَمٍ
وَرَحْمَةٍ لِلَّذِي قَدْ تَابَ مِنْ زَلَلِ

I ask forgiveness of Allah! Allah possesses generosity
and mercy for the one who turns away from his error.

أَسْتَغْفِرُ اللهَ مِنْ ذَنْبٍ وَمِنْ زَلَلِ
وَمِنْ خَطَايَا وَمِنْ وَهْمٍ وَمِنْ أَمَلِ

I ask forgiveness of Allah for wrong actions and mistakes,
and for my errors, delusion and wishful thinking.

أَسْتَغْفِرُ اللهَ مِنْ كِبْرٍ وَمِنْ حَسَدٍ
وَمِنْ رِيَاءٍ لِأَهْلِ الْمَالِ بِالْعَمَلِ

I ask forgiveness of Allah for any pride and envy,
and for hypocritical behaviour towards the rich.

أَسْتَغْفِرُ اللهَ مِنْ ظَنٍّ قَبِيحٍ بَدَا

مِنْ رُؤْيَةِ النَّفْسِ عُجْبًا مِنْهَا بِالْحُلَلِ

I ask forgiveness of Allah for ugly thoughts which
emerge from seeing the self and admiring its form.

أَسْتَغْفِرُ اللهَ مِنْ غِلٍّ وَحِقْدٍ وَمَا

أَضْمَرْتُ فِي سَالِفِ الْأَعْمَارِ مِنْ عِلَلِ

I ask forgiveness of Allah for all malice and spite
and for the faults I concealed in my earlier years.

أَسْتَغْفِرُ اللهَ مِنْ نُطْقٍ بِفَاحِشَةٍ

وَمِنْ سُكُوتٍ عَنْ غِيبَةٍ وَعَنْ خَلَلِ

I ask forgiveness of Allah for saying dreadful things
and for being silent in the face of slander and injury to others.

أَسْتَغْفِرُ اللهَ مِنْ زُورٍ وَمِنْ كَذِبٍ

وَمِنْ غُرُورٍ يَجُرُّ النَّفْسَ لِلْكَسَلِ

I ask forgiveness of Allah for dishonesty and lying
and for self-delusion which leads the self to indolence.

أَسْتَغْفِرُ اللهَ مِنْ ذَنْبٍ بِجَارِحَةٍ

وَمِنْ حُقُوقٍ أَتَتْ لِلنَّاسِ مِنْ قِبَلِي

I ask forgiveness of Allah for wrong actions done with the limbs,
and for rights owed to people.

أَسْتَغْفِرُ اللهَ مِنْ عِلْمٍ أَزِيغُ بِهِ
عَنِ الصِّرَاطِ الْقَوِيمِ الْمُفْضِي لِلْوَجَلِ

I ask forgiveness of Allah for any knowledge by which I deviate
from the straight path that leads to fear.

أَسْتَغْفِرُ اللهَ مِنْ حَالٍ أَصُولُ بِهِ
وَمِنْ مَقَامٍ أَدَّىٰ لِلْخَوْفِ وَالْخَجَلِ

I ask forgiveness of Allah for any state which I rush into,
and for any station that leads to fear and confusion.

أَسْتَغْفِرُ اللهَ مِنْ فِعْلٍ بِلَا نِيَّةٍ
وَمِنْ ذُهُولٍ أَتَىٰ لِلْقَلْبِ عَنْ عَجَلِ

I ask forgiveness of Allah for any act done without intention
and for distraction which quickly overwhelms the heart.

أَسْتَغْفِرُ اللهَ مِنْ دَعْوَى الْحُلُولِ وَمِنْ
دَعْوَى اتِّحَادٍ أَدَّىٰ لِلزَّيْغِ وَالْفَشَلِ

I ask forgiveness of Allah for claiming incarnation
and for claiming fusion, as these claims lead to deviation and failure.

أَسْتَغْفِرُ اللهَ مِنْ دَعْوَى الْوُجُودِ وَمِنْ
إِثْبَاتِ شَيْءٍ سِوَى الْمَوْجُودِ فِي الْأَزَلِ

I ask forgiveness of Allah for claiming existence,
and for affirming anything other than the Existent in before-time.

158

أَسْتَغْفِرُ اللهَ مِنْ عَقَائِدَ طَرَأَتْ

قَدْ خَالَفَتْ مِنْهَاجَ الْمُخْتَارِ وَالرُّسُلِ

I ask forgiveness of Allah for beliefs that occur which are
contrary to the path of the Chosen One and the Messengers.

أَسْتَغْفِرُ اللهَ مِنْ جَهْلٍ وَمِنْ سَفَهٍ

وَمِنْ فُتُورٍ أَتَى لِلنَّفْسِ عَنْ مَلَلٍ

I ask forgiveness of Allah for ignorance and folly
and for the languor that comes to the self from boredom.

أَسْتَغْفِرُ اللهَ مِنْ فِكْرٍ أَجُولُ بِهِ

بِلَا اعْتِبَارٍ جَرَى فِي الْعُلْوِيِ وَالسُّفْلِ

I ask forgiveness of Allah for any thought, be it high or low,
that has occupied me without taking a reminder from it.

أَسْتَغْفِرُ اللهَ مِقْدَارَ الْعَوَالِمِ مِنْ

عَرْشٍ وَلَوْحٍ وَعُمْرِ سَائِرِ الدُّوَلِ

I ask forgiveness of Allah by the measure of the worlds of the Throne,
the Tablet of forms and the duration of every dynasty.

أَسْتَغْفِرُ اللهَ وَهَّابَ الْعَطَايَا لِمَنْ

قَدِ اتَّقَاهُ بِلَا حَوْلٍ وَلَا حِيَلٍ

I ask forgiveness of Allah, the Ceaseless Giver of gifts to all
who fear Him, being themselves unreservedly powerless.

أَسْتَغْفِرُ اللهَ مُعْطِي مَنْ يَلُوذُ بِهِ
مَعَارِفًا بِطُرُوقِ الْعِلْمِ وَالنَّحَلِ

I ask forgiveness of Allah Who grants gnoses in the paths of knowledge
and gifts, to whoever takes refuge with Him.

أَسْتَغْفِرُ اللهَ رَحْمَنَ الْخَلَائِقِ مِنْ
جِنٍّ وَإِنْسٍ وَأَمْلَاكٍ وَكُلِّ عَالِي

I ask forgiveness of Allah Who has compassion on all creatures:
jinn, men, angels, and every exalted one.

رَبِّ بِأَحْمَدَ كُنْ لِأَمْرِنَا وَلِيًّا
وَمُرْشِدًا لِاتِّبَاعِ أَقْوَمِ السُّبُلِ

My Lord, by Ahmad, be the Master of our affair
and the Guide in following the straightest of paths.

عَلَيْهِ أَزْكَىٰ صَلَاةِ اللهِ مَا هَطَلَتْ
غَيْثٌ وَمَا قَدْ سَرَىٰ فِي الاَرْضِ مِنْ بَلَلِ

May the purest of Allah's blessings be upon him
as long as rain pours down and waters flow in the earth.

كَذَاكَ آلَكَ وَالصَّحْبُ الْكِرَامُ وَمَنْ
قَدِ اقْتَفَىٰ إِثْرَهُمْ مِنْ مُتَّقٍ وَوَلِي ۝

And upon your family and noble Companions and all
who follow in their footsteps who have fear of Allah, and every Wali.

Departure of Illusion

تليها لامية

ارتحال الوهم

كَانَ لِي وَهْمٌ فَلَمَّا أَنْ رَحَلْ
أَشْرَفَ الْقَلْبُ عَلَىٰ نُورِ الازَلْ

I had an illusion. When it departed,
the heart looked upon the light of before-time.

رَكِبَ الشَّوْقَ الَّذِي طَارَ بِهِ
فَدَنَا مِنْ حِبِّهِ حَتَّى اتَّصَلْ

It rode on longing, which flew with it,
so the heart drew near to its Beloved until it was united.

شَاهَدَ الْكَوْنَ خَيَالًا زَائِلًا
وَانْمَحَىٰ رَسْمُ الْوُجُودِ وَأَفَـلْ

It saw created beings as an imagination that faded,
and the form of existence was obliterated and vanished.

ثُمَّ رُدَّ لِلْبَقَـاءِ مُثْبِتًا
جَمِيعَ الْكَوْنِ الَّذِي عَنْهُ انْعَزَلْ

Then it was returned to going-on, confirming
all the beings from which it had withdrawn.

جَمَعَ الضِّدَّيْنِ فِي مَشْهَدِهِ
وَحَّدَ اللهَ وَقَامَ بِالْعَمَـلْ

It joined the two opposites in witnessing Him;
it unified Allah and took on action.

حَازَ سِرًّا وَصِرَاطًا سَوِيًّا
قَلَّ مَنْ ذَاقَهُ مِنْ أَهْلِ الْكَمَـالْ

It gained a secret and a level path;
how few of the people of perfection taste it.

رَبَّنَا صَلِّ عَلَى النُّورِ الَّذِي
كُلُّ عَبْدٍ أَمَّهُ حَازَ الْامَـلْ

Our Lord, bless the light.
Every slave who reaches him gains his desire.

وَارْضَ عَنْ ءَالِهِ هُمْ أَهْلُ النُّهَىٰ
وَصِحَابٍ مَعَ قُطْبٍ وَبَدَلْ ۞

Be pleased with his family, they are the people of understanding;
and the Companions, the Qutb and the Abdal.

Eyewitnessing

وتليه نونية

الشهود والعيان

يَا مَنْ يُرِدْ حَضْرَةَ الْعِيَانِ

إِرْقَ عَنِ الرُّوحِ وَالاَوَانِي

O you who desire the presence of eyewitnessing,
ascend and rise above the spirit and the forms.

وَالْعَدَمَ الاَصْلِيَّ الْزَمَنْهُ

وَكُنْ كَأَنْ لَمْ تَكُنْ يَا فَانِي

And you must cling to the original void –
and be as if you were not, O annihilated!

تَرَىٰ بِسِرٍّ وُجُودًا حَقًّا

سَرَتْ مَعَانِيهْ فِي كُلِّ ءَانِ

Indeed you will see existence truly
by a secret whose meanings have spread in every age.

فَلَمْ يُعَدِّدْ ذَا الْفِعْلِ شَيْءٌ
مِنْ صُوَرِ الْفِعْلِ وَالْكِيَانِ

None of the many images of action and entity
multiply the Actor in any way.

فَمَنْ تَرَقَّى عَنْ كُلِّ فَانٍ
رَءَا وُجُودًا بِغَيْرِ ثَانٍ

So whoever rises above every vanishing thing
will see existence without any second.

يَا فَوْزَ مَنْ قَدْ غَدَا يُشَاهِدْ
رَبًّا عَطُوفًا حَلِيمًا دَانِي

Oh the victory of one who has come to witness
a Lord Who is compassionate, forbearing and near.

يَقْبَلُ مَنْ قَدْ أَتَى فَقِيرًا
قَدْ تَابَ مِنْ حَالِهِ الظُّلْمَانِي

He accepts whoever comes in need,
who has turned away from his own dark state.

فَتَوْبَةُ الْعَبْدِ تَصْطَفِيهِ
لِحَضْرَةِ الْحُبِّ وَالتَّدَانِي

The slave's turning away from wrong action
purifies him for the presence of love and drawing-near.

وَذِكْرُهُ مَعْ شُهُودِ فَضْلٍ

يُحَصِّلُ الْوَارِدَ النُّورَانِي

Dhikr of Allah while witnessing His overflowing
obtains for him a luminous awakening.

مَنْ كَانَ مِنْ نَفْسِهِ فِي أَمْنٍ

كَانَ مِنَ الْخَلْقِ فِي أَمَانٍ

Whoever is safe from his own self
is also safe from the creation.

نُخَالِفِ النَّفْسَ فِي هَوَاهَا

وَصَاحِبَنْ عَارِفًا رَبَّانِي

So oppose the self in its desires
and seek the company of a gnostic of Allah.

يُرِيكَ مِنْ عَيْبِهَا الْخَفِي

يُعَالِجَنْ بِالدَّوَا الرُّوحَانِي

He will point out to you your hidden faults
and will treat you with a spiritual remedy.

يَسْلُكُ بِالرِّفْقِ فِي الْمَسِيرِ

يَرْحَمُ أَهْلَ الْبَلَا وَالْجَانِي

He acts gently towards you on the journey
with compassion for the people of trial and the delinquent.

يُفْنِيكَ بِالذِّكْرِ فِي الْحَقِيقَهْ

يُذَكِّرُ الْقَلْبَ بِالْقُرْءَان

He annihilates you through dhikr in the reality;
he reminds the heart through the Qur'an.

يُرَوِّحُ الرُّوحَ بِالاِشَارَهْ

فَتَنْجَلِي عِنْدَهَا الْمَعَانِي

He refreshes the spirit through indications
so at that the meanings disclose themselves.

يَا رَبِّ صَلِّ عَلَى النَّبِيِّ

مَا تُلِيَتْ سُورَةُ الْمَثَانِي

O Lord, bless the Prophet
as long as Surat al-Mathani is recited,

وَءَالِهِ وَالصَّحَابِ طُرًّا

مَا رَبِحَ النَّاسُ بِالاِيمَانِ

And his family and all of the Companions
as long as people profit by Iman.

وَأَطْلُبُ الْحَقَّ فِي السَّعَادَهْ

لِكُلِّ مَنْ ضَمَّهُ زَمَانِي ۝

I ask the Truly Real for bliss
for all whom my age comprises.

166

The Oneness of Action and Existence

وله رضي الله عنه رائية
وحدة الفعل والوجود

سَأَلْتُ قَلْبِي عَنْ قُرْبِ رَبِّي
فَقَالَ لَا شَكَّ هُوَ حَاضِرْ

I asked my heart about the nearness of my Lord,
so it said, 'There is no doubt that He is present.'

فَقُلْتُ مَا لِيَ لَا أَرَاهُ
فَقَالَ لِي هُوَ فِيكَ ظَاهِرْ

I said, 'What is wrong with me that I do not see Him?'
And it said to me, 'He is manifest in you.'

فَقُلْتُ هَـٰذَا الْاَمْرُ عَجِيبُ
فَكَيْفَ يَخْفَىٰ وَالنُّورُ بَاهِرْ

I said, 'This is truly astonishing –
how can He be hidden when light is brilliant?'

فَقَالَ وَهْمٌ هُوَ الْحِجَابُ

وَهْوَ لِكُلِّ الاَنَامِ قَاهِرْ

So it said, 'It is illusion that is the veil:
and it overpowers each and every one.'

لَكِنَّ مَنْ كَانَ ذَا اجْتِبَاءِ

غَابَ عَنِ الْوَهْمِ بِالسَّرَائِرْ

'However, the one who is chosen
withdraws from illusion through his secrets.

وَصَارَ رُوحًا بِغَيْرِ جِسْمٍ

وَشَاهَدَ الرَّبَّ بِالْبَصَائِرْ

'And he becomes a spirit without body
and directly sees the Lord with inner sight.'

فَغَايَةُ الفَتْحِ فِي الشُّهُودِ

لِحَضْرَةٍ مَا لَهَا مِنْ سَاتِرْ

So the goal of opening in vision
is a Presence that has no veil.

فَلَيْسَ فِعْلٌ وَلَا وُجُودٌ

لِغَيْرِ رَبِّي عِنْدَ الاَكَابِرْ

For the great there is neither action
nor existence from other than my Lord.

فَكُلُّ مَنْ بَاحَ بِاخْتِيَارٍ

مِنْ غَيْرِ إِذْنٍ لَهُ الزَّوَاجِرْ

Whoever divulges the Secret by choice,
without Idhn, has restrictions placed on him.

يَا رَبِّ إِفْتَحْ لَنَا الْبَصَائِرْ

وَنُوِّرِ الْقَلْبَ وَالسَّرَائِرْ

O Lord, open our inner sight for us
and illumine our heart and our secret.

ثُمَّ الصَّلَاةُ عَلَى النَّبِيِّ

مَا جَدَّ حِبٌّ وَسَارَ سَائِرْ

Then bless the Prophet as long as there is a lover
serious in his love and a wayfarer journeying.

وَءَالِهِ وَالصِّحَابِ جَمْعًا

مَا طَارَ شَوْقًا لِلَّه طَائِرْ ۝

And his family and Companions altogether,
as long as there is one who flies to Allah with longing.

Counsel

وتليه عينية

النصح

سَلَامٌ عَلَى الاِخْوَانِ فِي كُلِّ مَوْضِعٍ
سَلَامًا يَعُمُّ الْكُلَّ فِي كُلِّ مَجْمَعَ

Peace be upon the brothers in every place
— a peace that embraces all in every assembly.

وَإِنِّي أُرِيدُ النُّصْحَ لِلْكُلِّ رَاجِيًا
بُلُوغَ الْمُنَى وَالْعِزِّ وَالْفَتْحِ وَالْوُسْعِ

I wish to give good counsel to all, hoping
to obtain desire, might, the opening and strength.

فَأَوَّلُ نُصْحِي لِلَّذِي حَرَّرَ التَّقْوَىٰ
مُصَاحَبَةُ الاَخْيَارِ فِي الْجَلْبِ وَالدَّفْعِ

My first counsel for those dedicated to Taqwa
is to accompany the best in attracting and repulsing.

فَهَذَا أَسَاسُ الْخَيْرِ إِنْ كُنْتَ عَاقِلًا

فَعَوِّلْ عَلَيْهِ مَعْ مُرَاعَاةٍ لِلشَّرْعِ

For this is the basis of all good if you are intelligent;
so rely on it, along with being mindful of the Shari'a.

وَكُلُّ الَّذِي قَدْ نَالَ عِلْمًا وَسُؤْدَدًا

فَمَا نَالَهُ إِلَّا بِصُحْبَةِ خَاشِعٍ

All those who have obtained knowledge and mastery
have only obtained them by accompanying a humble man.

وَأَعْنِي بِهِ الشَّيْخَ الَّذِي فَاضَ نُورُه

وَجَاءَ بِأَسْرَارٍ وَخَيْرٍ مُتَابِعِ

By him I mean the Shaykh whose light has overflowed,
and who has brought secrets and uninterrupted good with him.

فَإِنْ شِئْتَ أَنْوَارًا وَفَتْحَ بَصِيرَةٍ

فَقَلِّدْهُ تَعْظِيمًا وَعِجْ عَنْ مُنَازِعِ

If you desire lights and the opening of inner sight,
then copy him in exalting Allah and turn from people of conflict.

وَوَاظِبْ عَلَى الذِّكْرِ الْمُلَقَّنِ بِالْإِذْنِ

وَلَا تَغْفُلَنْ فِي حَالَةِ الضِّيقِ وَالْوُسْعِ

And persevere in the dhikr taught through Idhn
and neglect it neither in constriction nor expansion.

وَزِنْ وَارِدَاتِ الذِّكْرِ بِالشَّرْعِ حَاكِيًا

لِشَيْخِكَ كُلَّ مَا أَتَاكَ وَسَارِعِ

Weigh the luminous openings of the dhikr with the Shari'a,
telling your Shaykh quickly all that happens to you.

فَسَلْبُ اخْتِيَارٍ ثُمَّ كُلِّ إِرَادَةٍ

هُوَ المَوْرِدُ الاَصْفَىٰ فَهَلْ أَنْتَ سَامِعِ

So the negation of choice, and then all will,
is the purest of springs, if you are able to hear.

وَهَاكَ مَقَامَاتِ الْيَقِينِ فَبَادِرَنْ

بِتَوْبَةٍ زُهْدٍ ثُمَّ خَوْفٍ بِوَازِعِ

These are the Stations of Certainty – hasten to tawba,
doing-without, and then fear which brings restraint.

رَجَاءٍ وَشُكْرٍ ثُمَّ صَبْرٍ تَوَكُّلٍ

كَذَاكَ الرِّضَىٰ وَالْحُبُّ لِلْكُلِّ جَامِعِ

Hope, gratitude, then patience and putting your trust in Allah,
similarly contentment, and love unites them all.

وَأَسْبَابُهُ الْفِكْرُ الصَّفِيُّ فِي نِعْمَةٍ

وَحُسْنِ صِفَاتٍ ثُمَّ فِي النُّورِ اللَّامِعِ

Its causes are the pure contemplation of blessing and of
the perfection of the Attributes, then of the dazzling light.

وَأَعْنِي بِهِ ذَاكَ الرَّسُولَ مُحَمَّدًا

عَلَيْهِ صَلَاةٌ عَدَّ وَتْرٍ مَعَ الشَّفْعِ

By it, I mean that Messenger Muhammad,
may blessings be upon him in quantity as great as all that is even or odd,

وَءَالِهِ وَالْاَصْحَابِ مَعْ كُلِّ عَارِفٍ

دَعَا لِطَرِيقِ اللهِ فِي كُلِّ مُجْمَعٍ ۞

And on his family and Companions and every gnostic,
calling to the path of Allah in every assembly.

Annihilation in Allah

وتليه هائية

الفناء في الله

يَا طَالِبَ الْفَنَا فِي اللّٰه

قُلْ دَائِمًا اَللّٰه اَللّٰه

O seeker of annihilation in Allah,
say constantly, 'Allah! Allah!'

وَغِبْ فِيهِ عَنْ سِواهْ

وَاشْهَدْ بِقَلْبِكَ اَللّٰه

And withdraw into Him from other-than-Him,
and with your heart – witness Allah.

وَاجْمَعْ هُمُومَكَ فِيهِ

تُكْفَىٰ بِهِ عَنْ غَيرِ اللّٰه

Gather your concerns in Him and He will be
enough in place of other-than-Allah.

174

وَكُنْ عَبْدًا صِرْفًا لَهُ

تَكُنْ حُرًّا عَنْ غَيْرِ اللّٰهْ

Be a pure slave to Him and
you will be free from other-than-Allah.

وَاخْضَعْ لَهُ وَتَذَلَّلْ

تَفُزْ بِسِرٍّ مِنَ اللّٰهْ

Submit to Him and humble yourself
and you will win a secret from Allah.

وَاذْكُرْ بِجِدٍّ وَصِدْقٍ

بَيْنَ يَدَيْ عَبِيدِ اللّٰهْ

Do dhikr with intensity and sincerity in the
presence of the slaves of Allah.

وَاكْتُمْ إِذَا تَجَلَّىٰ لَكَ

بِأَنْوَارٍ مِنْ ذَاتِ اللّٰهْ

Conceal it when He manifests Himself to you
with lights from the Essence of Allah.

فَالْغَيْرُ عِنْدَنَا مُحَالْ

فَالْوُجُودُ الْحَقُّ لِلّٰهْ

With us, other is impossible,
for true existence belongs to Allah.

وَوَهْمَكَ اقْطَعْ دَائِمًا

بِتَوْحِيدٍ صِرْفٍ لِلَّه

Constantly cut through your illusion
with a Tawhid that is purely for Allah.

فَوَحْدَةُ الْفِعْلِ تَبْدُو

فِي أَوَّلِ الذِّكْرِ لِلَّه

The oneness of action appears
at the beginning of dhikr of Allah.

وَوَحْدَةُ الْوَصْفِ لَه

تَاتِي مِنَ الْحُبِّ فِي اللّه

And the oneness of His attributes
comes from love for the sake of Allah.

وَوَحْدَةُ الذَّاتِ لَه

تُورِّثُ الْبَقَا بِاللّه

And the oneness of His Essence
gives going-on by Allah.

فَهَنِيئًا لِمَنْ مَشَىٰ

فِي طَرِيقِ الذِّكْرِ لِلَّه

Joy to the one who walks
on the path of dhikr for the sake of Allah,

مُعْتَقِدًا شَيْخًا حَيًّا

يَكُونُ عَارِفًا بِاللهْ

believing in a living Shaykh
who is a gnostic of Allah.

وَلَازِمَ الْحُبَّ لَهُ

وَبَاعَ نَفْسَهُ لِلَّهْ

He holds constantly to His love
and sells his self to Allah.

وَقَامَ فِي اللَّيْلِ يَتْلُو

كَلَامَهُ شَوْقًا لِلَّهْ

He rises in the night to recite His word,
longing for Allah.

فَنَالَ مَا يَطْلُبُهْ

مِنْ قُوَّةِ الْعِلْمِ بِاللهْ

He gets what he seeks of the power
of knowledge of Allah.

وَفَيْضُنَا مِنْ نَبِيٍّ

سَيِّدُ مَخْلُوقَاتِ اللهْ

Our gifts are from a Prophet who is the
master of the creatures of Allah.

عَلَيْهِ أَزْكَىٰ صَلَاةٍ

عَدَدَ مَعْلُومَاتِ اللهْ

May the purest of blessings be upon him
in quantity as great as the things known to Allah.

وَءَالِهِ وَصَحْبِهِ

وَكُلِّ دَاعٍ إِلَى اللهْ ۞

And his family and Companions,
And everyone who calls to Allah.

Withdrawal from Other Than Allah

وتليه هائية

الغيبة عما سوى الله

رُوحِي تُحَدِّثُنِي بِأَنَّ حَقِيقَتِي

نُورُ الإلَهِ فَلَا تَرَىٰ إِلَّاهُ

My spirit tells me, "My reality is the light of Allah,
so see no one but Him."

لَوْ لَمْ أَكُنْ نُورًا لَكُنْتُ سِوَاءَهُ

إِنَّ السِّوَا عَدَمٌ فَلَا تَرْضَاهُ

If I were not a light I would be other-than-Him.
Indeed otherness is nothingness, so do not be content with it.

وَإِذَا نَظَرْتَ بِعَيْنِ سِرِّكَ لَمْ تَجِدْ

غَيْرَ الإلَهِ فِي أَرْضِهِ وَسَمَاهُ

If you look with the eye of your Secret you will not find
a trace of other-than-Allah in either His earth or His heaven.

لَكِنْ تَوَهُّمُ غَيْرِهِ يَخْفَى بِهِ

فَانْبُذْ هَوَاكَ إِذَا أَرَدْتَ تَرَاهُ

But the illusion of other-than-Him hides Him.
So combat your desires if you wish to see Him.

وَارْكَبْ سَفِينَةَ سُنَّةٍ تَنْجُو بِهَا

وَاسْلُكْ سَبِيلَ رَئِيسِهَا فِي هَوَاهُ

Board the ship of the Sunna and you will be rescued by it,
and travel the path of its captain in his love.

وَصِلِ الشَّرَابَ بِكَأْسِهَا وَافْنَى بِهِ

تَحُزِ الْبَقَاءَ بِسِرِّهِ وَعَلَاهُ

Unite the wine with the goblet and be annihilated by it,
and you will obtain going-on by His secret and sublimity.

وَاشْهَدْ بِعَيْنِ بَصِيرَةٍ تَوْحِيدَهُ

وَالْفَرْقُ شِرْعَتُهُ فَلَا تَنْسَاهُ

See His Tawhid with the eye of inner sight,
but separation is His Shari'a so do not forget it!

وَاجْعَلْ هُمُومَكَ وَاحِدًا تُكْفَى بِهِ

كُلَّ الْهُمُومِ وَتَدْخُلَنْ فِي حِمَاهُ

Make your concerns one, and by Him all your needs
will be met, and you will enter into His protection.

وَانْزِلْ أُمُورَكَ بِالَّذِي أَدْرَىٰ بِهَا

فَهُوَ الْخَبِيرُ بِقَلْبِنَا وَمُنَاهُ

Hand over your affairs to the One Who knows them best,
for He is the Aware Who knows our hearts and their desires.

يَا رَبِّ صَلِّ عَلَى النَّبِيِّ مُحَمَّدٍ

سِرِّ الْوُجُودِ وَأَصْلِهِ وَسَنَاهُ ﴿﴾

O Lord, bless the Prophet Muhammad,
the secret of existence and its source and splendour.

Manifestation of the Essence

وتليه هائية

التجلي

أَشَمْسٌ بَدَا مِنْ عَالَمِ الْغَيْبِ ضَوْؤُهَا

أَمِ انْكَشَفَتْ عَنْ ذَاتِ لَيْلَى سُتُورُهَا

Has the light of the sun appeared from the world of the Unseen,
or have the veils of Layla been lifted from Her essence?

نَعَمْ تِلْكَ لَيْلَى قَدْ أَبَاحَتْ بِحُبِّهَا

لِخِلٍّ لَهَا لَمَّا تَزَايَدَ شَوْقُهَا

Yes, Layla revealed Her love
for Her intimate friend when Her longing grew.

فَأَضْحَى أَسِيرًا فِي مُرَادِ غَرَامِهَا

وَنَادَتْ لَهُ الْاشْوَاقُ هَذِي كُؤُوسُهَا

He became a captive of Her ardent desire
and the longings which are Her goblets called out to him.

فَمَا بَرِحَتْ حَتَّى سَقَتْهُ بِكَأْسِهَا
فَلَا لَوْمَ فَاشْرَبْ فَالشَّرَابُ حَدِيثُهَا

She did not leave until She had given him a drink from Her goblet.
There is no blame. Drink – for the wine is Her speech.

وَمَا هِيَ إِلَّا حَضْرَةُ الْحَقِّ وَحْدَهَا
تَجَلَّتْ بِأَشْكَالٍ تَلَوَّنَ نُورُهَا

She is none but the Presence of the Truth alone,
Who manifests Herself with forms whose every light is different.

فَأَبْدَتْ بَدِيعَ الصُّنْعِ فِي طَيِّ كَوْنِهَا
فَلَاحِظْ صِفَاتِ الْحِبِّ فِيكَ ظُهُورُهَا

In folding up Her cosmos, She showed the Originator of the design,
so look how the Attributes of the Beloved are manifest within you.

فَوَاللهِ مَا حَازَ السَّعَادَةَ كُلَّهَا
سِوَى مَنْ بَدَا عَبْدًا ذَلِيلًا يَؤُمُّهَا

By Allah, no one ever obtains complete bliss
except one who becomes a humble slave and seeks Her out.

فَغَطَّتْ قَبِيحَ الْوَصْفِ مِنْهُ بِوَصْفِهَا
وَلَاحَتْ لَهُ الأَنْوَارُ يَبْدُو شُعَاعُهَا

She covered the ugliness of his attributes with the beauty of Hers,
and lights shone from him, their rays appearing.

فَغَابَ عَنِ الْحِسِّ الَّذِي كَانَ قَاطِعًا

وَعَانَقَ مَعْنًى لَا يَحِلُّ فِرَاقُهَا

He withdrew from the sensory which is a barrier
and embraced a meaning from which it is unlawful to be separated.

فَحَرِّرْ أَخِي قَصْدًا وَأَعْرِضْ عَنِ السِّوَىٰ

يَهُبُّ عَلَى الاَحْبَابِ مِنْكَ نَسِيمُهَا

Let your goal be to commit yourself, brother, and avoid otherness,
and Her breeze will waft over the lovers from you.

وَتَفْتَحُ سَمْعًا لِلْفُؤَادِ مِنْ سَالِكٍ

لِأَنَّ لَطِيفَ الْعِلْمِ مِنْهَا دَلِيلُهَا

You will open the hearing of the wayfarer's heart because
the all-pervading nature of the knowledge from Her is proof of Her.

فَمُنَّ عَلَيْنَا دَائِمًا بِوِصَالِهَا

وَغِيبْنَا عَنْ حِسِّ الْمَوْجُودَاتِ كُلِّهَا ۞

Bestow on us always the blessing of union with Her
and make us withdraw from every existent thing.

184

Purification

وتليها واوية

التطهير

فَإِنْ شِئْتَ تَطْهِيرًا مِنَ الشِّرْكِ وَالدَّعْوَىٰ

وَتَشْرَبَ مِنْ تَسْنِيمٍ وَصْلٍ حَتَّىٰ تَرْوَىٰ

If you wish purification from shirk and the claim that you exist,
and to drink from the nectar of union until you are quenched –

فَمِنْطِقْ بِصَبْرٍ ثُمَّ عَمِّمْ بِتَوْبَةٍ

وَلَازِمْ قَمِيصَ الزُّهْدِ وَابْذُلْ فِيهِ قُوَىٰ

– then wrap yourself in patience and wind on the turban of Tawba.
Wear the shirt of doing-without and in it exhaust your strength.

وَلَا بُدَّ مِنْ نَعْلَيْنِ خَوْفٍ مَعَ الرَّجَىٰ

وَعُكَّازِ إِيقَانٍ وَزَادٍ مِنَ التَّقْوَىٰ

The twin sandals of fear and hope are indispensable.
Take the staff of certainty and a store of Taqwa.

وَقَائِدُ عِلْمٍ مَعْ مَطِيَّةِ هِمَّةٍ

وَصُحْبَةِ حِفْظٍ لِلْجَوَارِحِ مِنْ بَلْوَىٰ

Take the bridle of knowledge for the horse of Himma, and the
protection of companions who will guard the limbs from trials.

بِجُدَّ وَأَسْرِعْ فِي الْمَسِيرِ وَلَا تَقِفْ

بِفِكْرٍ عَلَىٰ كَوْنٍ فَتُحْجَبَ عَنْ مَأْوَىٰ

Struggle seriously and travel quickly on the journey.
Do not stop to think about the universe, and so be barred from refuge.

وَفَكِّرْ فِي إِحْسَانٍ وَأَخْلِصْ فِي شُكْرِهِ

وَقُمْ سَحَراً وَاخْضَعْ وَبُثَّ لَهُ الشَّكْوَىٰ

Rather reflect on Ihsan and be sincere in gratitude to Him,
and get up before dawn, submit, and hand over your complaint to Him.

وَصَلِّ عَلَىٰ قُطْبِ الْوُجُودِ وَحِزْبِهِ

صَلَاةً تَعُمُّ السِّرَّ مِنَّا مَعَ النَّجْوَىٰ ۞

Bless the Qutb of existence and his group with a blessing
that will spread the Secret from us.

Counsel on Death

للشيخ سيدي محمد ابن الحبيب

تَزَوَّدْ أَخِي لِلْمَوْتِ إِنَّهُ نَازِلٌ
وَلَا تُطِلِ الآمَالَ يَقْسُوا لَكَ الْقَلْبُ

Prepare yourself for death, O my brother, for it will descend.
Do not draw out your hopes, in case your heart becomes hard.

وَوَاظِبْ عَلَى الْفِكْرِ الْمُعِينِ عَلَى الْجِدّ
وَسَارِعْ إِلَى الاَعْمَالِ فَالْعُمْرُ يَذْهَبُ

Persevere in reflection which will make you aware
and move you to do good works, for life will soon depart.

وَفَكِّرْ فِي أَحْوَالِ الْقِيَامَة دَائِمًا
كَبَعْثٍ وَنَشْرٍ وَالْمَوَازِينُ تُنْصَبُ

Constantly reflect on the states of the Last Hour, the Rising,
the Gathering and the Balance of actions which is set up.

وَكَالصِّرَاطِ الَّذِي لَهُ عَقَبَاتُهُ
تَطُولُ عَلَى الْعَاصِي وَمَشْيُهُ يَصْعُبُ

Then there is the Bridge which has its steep and difficult ascents;
it will be lengthy for the disobedient and walking on it will be hard,

وَمَنْ كَانَ طَائِعًا وَلِلَّهِ مُخْلِصًا
يَمُرُّ كَبَرْقٍ أَوْ كَرِيحٍ فَيَذْهَبُ

while whoever was obedient and sincere towards Allah
will pass over it like lightning or a wind and will go on.

وَإِنْ شِئْتَ أَنْ تُسْقَىٰ مِنَ الْحَوْضِ فِي الْحَشْرِ
فَلَازِمْ حُبَّ النَّبِي وَمَنْ لَهُ يُنْسَبُ

If you wish to be given a drink from the Basin on the Day of Gathering,
you must love the Prophet and his descendants.

وَصَلِّ عَلَى الْهَادِي الْمُشَفَّعِ فِي الْوَرَىٰ
فَهُوَ الَّذِي لَهَا إِذَا انْخَلْقُ يَرْهَبُ

And bless the Guide whose intercession for mankind is accepted,
for he is the one who intercedes when people are terrified.

عَلَيْهِ صَلَاةُ اللهِ فِي كُلِّ مَوْطِنٍ
وَءَالٍ وَأَصْحَابٍ وَمَنْ يَتَحَبَّبُ

May the blessings of Allah be upon him in every land,
and on his family and Companions and those who show love for him.

وَأَسْأَلُ رَبِّ اللهَ نَيْلَ سَعَادَةٍ

لِي وَلِلْأَحْبَابِ وَمَنْ يَتَقَرَّبُ ﴿۝﴾

I ask my Lord, Allah, for the gift of true happiness
for me and the beloved ones and those who draw near.

Another Song

أَهِيمُ وَحْدِي بِذِكْرِ رَبِّي
فَذِكْرُ رَبِّي هُوَ الشِّفَاءُ

I am ecstatic, alone, in the dhikr of my Lord,
for the dhikr of my Lord – it is the cure.

أَحْبَبْتُ رَبًّا هُوَ اِعْتِمَادِي
لِكُلِّ شَيْءٍ هُوَ يَشَاءُ

I have loved a Lord – on Whom I rely;
in each single thing – it is He Who wills it.

وَكُلُّ حُبٍّ لِغَيْرِ رَبِّي
فِيهِ الْعَذَابُ فِيهِ الشَّقَاءُ

In every love for other than my Lord
there is torment and grief.

190

يَا فَوْزَ فَانٍ عَنِ الْفَنَاءِ

لَهُ الْحَيَاةُ لَهُ الْبَقَاءُ

Oh the victory of the one annihilated to annihilation,
he will have life and going on.

يَا رَبِّ صَلِّ عَلَى مُحَمَّدْ

مِنْ ذَاتِهِ النُّورُ وَالضِّيَاءُ

O my Lord, bless Muhammad.
From his essence there is light and radiance.

وَءَالِهِ وَالصَّحْبِ الْكِرَامِ

لَهُمْ عُهُودٌ لَهُمْ وَفَاءُ ﴿﴾

And bless his family and noble Companions.
They have covenants; they fulfil them.

Song on Departure

قصيدة تذكر عند ختام
كل جلسة من جلسات الفقراء

كَمْ لَكَ مِنْ نِعْمَةٍ عَلَيَّ
وَلَمْ تَزَلْ مُحْسِناً إِلَيَّ

How many blessings You grant me
and You are continually good to me.

غَدَّيْتَنِي فِي الْحَشَا جَنِينَا
وَكُنْتَ لِي قَبْلَ وَالِدَيَّ

You fed me as an embryo in the womb
and You were mine before my parents.

خَلَقْتَنِي مُسْلِمًا وَلَوْ لَا
فَضْلُكَ لَمْ أَعْرِفِ النَّبِيَّ

You created me Muslim and had it not been for Your gift,
I would not have known the Prophet.

أَسْجُدُ حَقًّا عَلَى جَبِينِي
نَعَمْ وَخَدَّيْ وَنَاظِرَيَّا

In truth I prostrate on my forehead —
yes, and on my cheeks and eyes.

يَا رَبِّ صَلِّ عَلَى النَّبِيّ
مَا تُلِيَتْ سُورَةُ الْمَثَانِي

O Lord, bless the Prophet
as long as the Surat al-Mathani is recited.

وَءَالِهِ وَالصِّحَابِ طُرًّا
مَا رَبِحَ النَّاسُ بِالْإِيمَانِ

And his family and all the Companions,
as long as people profit by Iman.

وَأَطْلُبُ الْحَقَّ فِي السَّعَادَه
لِكُلِّ مَنْ ضَمَّهُ زَمَانِي ۞

I ask of the Real good fortune
for all whom my age comprises.

The Final Song

وهذا ما دعت الحاجة لذكره،

وأما الأمداح في جناب هذا الهيكل الصمدانى

العلامة الرباني فلا تعد ولا تحصى كثرة اه

سَلامٌ عَلَىٰ أَهْلِ الْحِمَىٰ حَيْثُمَا حَلُّوا

هَنِيئًا لَهُمْ يَا حَبَّذَا مَا بِهِ حَلُّوا

Peace be upon the People of the sanctuary wherever they alight.
May they enjoy it! How excellent the place where they stay.

لَهُمْ أَظْهَرَ الْمَوْلَىٰ شُمُوسَ بَهَائِه

فَيَا لَيْتَ خَدِّي فِي التُّرَابِ لَهُمْ نَعْلُ

For them, the Lord has manifested the suns of His splendour.
Would that my cheek were a sandal for them in the dust!

مَتَىٰ يَا عُرَيْبَ الْحَيِّ يَاتِي بَشِيرُكُمْ

فَتَبْتَهِجَ الدُّنيَا وَيَجْتَمِعَ الشَّمْلُ

When, dear brothers, will the herald bring good news of you
so that the world can celebrate and be reunited?

صِلُونِي عَلَىٰ مَا بِي فَإِنِّي لِوَصْلِكُمْ

إِذَا لَمْ أَكُنْ أَهْلًا فَأَنْتُمْ لَهُ أَهْلُ

Make our bond of love close in spite of what is inside me,
for if I do not deserve it, you are worthy of it.

سَلَامٌ عَلَيْكُمْ شَرَّفَ اللهُ قَدْرَكُمْ

وَدَامَتْ عَلَيْكُمْ نِعْمَةٌ وَسُرُورُهَا

Peace be upon you, may Allah exalt your rank,
and may the joy of blessings be upon you always.

فَمَا طَابَتِ الْأَيَّامُ إِلَّا بِذِكْرِكُمْ

فَأَنْتُمْ ضِيَاءُ الْعَيْنِ حَقًّا وَنُورُهَا

The days are joyless without your dhikr,
for truly you are the illumination of the eye and its light.

إِذَا نَظَرَتْ عَيْنِي وُجُوهَ أَحِبَّتِي

فَتِلْكَ صَلَاتِي فِي اللَّيَالِي الرَّغَائِبِ

When my eye looks on the faces of my beloved friends
that is my prayer during the longed-for nights.

وُجُوهٌ إِذَا مَا أَسْفَرَتْ عَنْ جَمَالِهَا

أَضَاءَتْ لَهَا الْأَكْوَانُ مِنْ كُلِّ جَانِبٍ ﴿﴾

They are such faces that when they shine, from their beauty
they light up the whole world.

Qasida of Ahmad al-Badawi

هذه قصيدة الشيخ سيدي احمد البدوي الفاسي

إِلَاهِي ضَاقَتِ الصُّدُورُ مِنَّا
فَثَبِّتْنَا وَأَيِّدْنَا تَأْيِيدَا

My God, our breasts are constricted,
so strengthen us and help us.

إِلَاهِي حَارَتِ الاَلْبَابُ مِنَّا
فَمَكِّنَّا وَرَقِّنَا الصُّعُودَا

My God, our minds are confused,
so make us firm and raise us to the heights.

إِلَاهِي عَنْ سِوَاكَ اقْطَعْ رَجَانَا
وَمِنْ بَحْرِ المُنَا فَاجْعَلْ وُرُودَا

My God, cut off our hopes from other-than-You,
and let us drink from the sea of raja'.

فَأَنْتَ نَصِيرِي وَالْمُعِينُ حَقًّا

وَفِيكَ رَجَاؤُنَا فَقِنَا الصُّدُودَا

Truly You are my helper and aid.
Our hopes lie with You, so keep us from rejection.

فَإِنَّ الدِّينَ أَمْرُهُ عَظِيمٌ

فَوَفِّقْنَا وَأَكْفِنَا الْوَعِيدَا

The Deen is a vast matter,
so give us success and fulfil the promise.

وَإِنَّ الْوَقْتَ قَدْ أَهَالَ فَأَحْسِنْ

لَنَا الْعُقْبَى وَكُنْ لَنَا رَشِيدَا

The moment has come, so be kind to us
in its results and be our guide.

وَتَوِّجْنَا بِفَرْدِيَّةٍ عَظِيمَهْ

وَأَجْعَلْ مِنْكَ رَبِّ لَنَا الْمَزِيدَا

Crown us with a tremendous uniqueness,
and, O Lord, give us increase from You,

أَفِضْ مَدَدًا لَنَا فِي كُلِّ قُطْرِ

وَلِلاَحْبَابِ سَهِّلِ الْوُرُودَا

Pour out help upon us from every quarter
and make the arrival easy for the lovers.

فَيَا فَرْدُ يَا صَمَدُ مُعِزٌّ

لِحِصْنِ الْمَجْدِ أَدْخِلَنْ فَرِيدَا

O Self-sufficient, the Goal, the Enhancer!
Bring us alone into the fortress of glory.

وَيَا قَهَّارُ فَاحْمِنَا بِقَهْرٍ

فَأَنْتَ نَصِيرُ مَنْ أَتَىٰ وَحِيدَا

And, O Ever-compelling, protect us with Your force
for You are the helper of whoever comes alone.

فَيَا جَبَّارُ فَاجْبِرْنَا بِخَيْرٍ

وَيَا رَزَّاقُ هَبْ رِزْقًا مَدِيدَا

O Irresistible, help us with the good,
and O Provider, give us adequate provision.

بِعِزِّكَ يَا عَزِيزُ احْرُسْ مَقَامِي

وَوَفِّقْ رَبِّ جَبَّارًا عَنِيدَا

O Almighty, guard my station with Your might,
and O Lord, bring the stubborn tyrant to agreement.

بِحَقِّكَ يَا مُهَيْمِنُ سَلِّمْ أَمْرِي

وَكُنْ يَا رَبِّ لِي رُكْنًا شَدِيدَا

O Protector, protect my affair with Your truth,
and O Lord, be a strong support for me.

كَبِيرُ يَا قَوِيُّ يَا مَتِينُ
وَيَا قَيُّومُ صُنْ سِرّشِي الْوَحِيدَا

O Great, Overpoweringly strong, Firm!
O Self-Subsisting, keep my secret, alone.

وَأَبْدِلْ بِدْعَةً بِكُلِّ هَدْيٍ
وَحَقِّقْنَا لِنُدْرِكَ الشُّهُودَا

Replace bida' with every guidance,
and grant us realisation so we may perceive the witnessing.

وَأَمِّنْ خَوْفَنَا وَاقْبَلْ دُعَانَا
فَحَاشَاكَ أَنْ تُخَيِّبَ الْمُرِيدَا

Give us safety from our fear and accept our supplication,
far be it from You that You should disappoint the murid.

بِخَاتِمَةٍ لَنَا فَاخْتِمْ عَظِيمَهْ
وَنَسْلِي كُلَّهُ فَاجْعَلْ سَعِيدَا

Grant us with a mighty seal at the end,
and make all my children fortunate.

بِجَاهِ الْمُصْطَفَىٰ وَالآلِ مَنْ قَدْ
بِهِ نَالُوا السَّعَادَةَ وَالْمَزِيدَا

By the rank of the Chosen One and his family and all
who have won happiness and increase through him.

بِأَصْحَابِهِ وَمَنْ تَبِعُوا وَأَسَّوْا
بِنَاءَ الدِّينِ حَتَّىٰ غَدَا مَشِيدَا

By his Companions and those who followed him
and helped establish the Deen until it became strong —

لَهُمْ أُهْدِي الصَّلَاةَ بِكُلِّ لَفْظٍ
يُرَىٰ فِي الْحِسِّ وَالْمَعْنَىٰ فَرِيدَا

I bestow a prayer on them with every word
seen to be one in spiritual and material meaning.

وَيَتْبَعُهَا سَلَامٌ مُسْتَمِرٌّ
عَلَىٰ مَرِّ الزَّمَانِ يُرَىٰ جَدِيدَا

The prayer is followed by peace extending throughout time,
yet seen to be renewed over the passage of time.

صَلَاةً تَمْلَأُ الْأَكْوَانَ نُورًا
وَتُسْعِدُ وَقْتَنَا فَيَكُونُ عِيدَا

It is a prayer which fills beings with light,
and makes our age happy so that it becomes a festival,

وَيَظْهَرُ خَيْرُهَا فَنَفُوزُ فَوْزًا
عَظِيمًا وَافِرَ الْمَعْنَىٰ مَدِيدَا

whose goodness is clearly manifest,
so we win a great victory full of vastness and meaning.

تَشَفَّعْ يَا رَسُولَ اللهِ فِينَا

فَمَا نَرْجُو الشَّفَاعَةَ مِنْ سِوَاكَا

O Messenger of Allah, intercede for us,
we do not hope for intercession from anyone except you.

أَغِثْ يَا خَيْرَ خَلْقِ اللهِ قَوْمًا

ضِعَافًا ظِلُّهُمْ أَبَدًا لِوَاكَا

O Best of Allah's creation, grant help
to a weak people whose protection is always your banner.

وَأَسْرِعْ فِي إِغَاثَتِنَا فَإِنَّا

نَرَى الْمَوْلَىٰ يُسَارِعُ فِي رِضَاكَا

Hasten to aid us, for we see
that the Lord is swift to approve of you.

عَلَيْكَ صَلَاةُ رَبِّنَا كُلَّ حِينٍ

وَآلِكَ كُلِّهِمْ وَمَنْ وَالَاكَا ۞

May the blessings of your Lord be upon you at every instant
and on all your family and those who are your friends.

202

The 99 Beautiful Names

هذه القصيدة الرائية في التوسّل بأسماء الله (تعالى) الحسنى
للسيد أحمد بن عبد العزيز الفيلاني

بَدَأْتُ بِبِسْمِ اللهِ في أَوَّلِ السَّطْرِ
فَأَسْمَاؤُهُ حِصْنٌ مَنِيعٌ مِنَ الضَّرِّ

I have begun with the name of Allah in the first line,
for His most Beautiful Names are a fortress invincible against harm.

وَصَلَّيْتُ في الثَّاني عَلَى خَيْرِ خَلْقِه
مُحَمَّدٍ المَبْعُوثِ بِالفَتحِ وَالنَّصرِ

In the second, I pray for blessings on the Best of Creation,
Muhammad, who was sent with an opening and triumph.

إِذَا اسْتَفْتَحَ القُرَّاءُ في مُحْكَمِ الذِّكْرِ
فَبِاسْمِكَ يَا ذَا العَرْشِ يَسْتَفْتِحُ المُقْرِئُ

When they begin in the circle of dhikr it is with Your name,
O Lord of the Throne, that the reciter must begin.

إِذَا نَابَنِي خَطْبٌ وَضَاقَ بِهِ صَدْرِي

تَلَافَاهُ لُطْفُ اللهِ مِنْ حَيْثُ لَا أَدْرِي

When I am in trouble and my breast constricts,
the lutf of Allah enters it, coming from where I do not know.

وَلَا سِيَّمَا إِذْ جِئْتُهُ مُتَوَسِّلًا

بِأَسْمَائِهِ الْحُسْنَى الْمُعَظَّمَةِ الْقَدْرِ

Especially when I come to Him, entreating Him
by His most beautiful and mighty Names.

فَيَا اللهُ يَا رَحْمَنُ إِنِّي لَذُو فَقْرٍ

وَأَنْتَ رَحِيمٌ مَالِكُ الْخَلْقِ وَالْاَمْرِ

So Allah, O All-Merciful, truly I am in dire poverty,
You are Compassionate, the Lord of Creation and the command.

بِقُدْسِكَ قُدُّوسٌ سَلَامٌ وَمُؤْمِنٌ

مُهَيْمِنٌ قَدِّسْنِي لَدَى السِّرِّ وَالْجَهْرِ

By Your purity, O Pure, O Peace, O Safety-giver,
O Protector, purify me both inside and outside.

عَزِيزٌ وَجَبَّارٌ وَيَا مُتَكَبِّرُ

وَيَا خَالِقَ الْخَلْقِ اكْفِنِي أَزْمَةَ الدَّهْرِ

O Hard of Access, Irresistible, Rightly Proud,
Creator of creation, shelter me on the Day of Reckoning.

204

وَيَا بَارِئُ مَالِي سِوَاكَ مُصَوِّرُ

وَغَفَّارُ يَا قَهَّارُ جَبْرًا لِذِى كَسْرِ

O first Creator and Giver of Form, I have none but You.
O Forgiving, O Compeller, mend the one who has been broken.

وَهَبْ لِي يَا وَهَّابُ رَزَّاقُ مَطْلَبِي

وَفَتَّاحُ أَشْرِقْ يَا عَلِيمُ دُجَىٰ فِكْرِي

O Giver, give me what I seek, O Provider.
O Opener, All-Knowing, illumine the darkness of my thoughts.

وَيَا قَابِضُ يَا بَاسِطُ خَافِضَ الْعِدَا

وَيَا رَافِعُ اِرْفَعْ بِالتِّبَاعِ الْهُدَىٰ ذِكْرِي

O He-Who-contracts, He-Who-expands, O Abaser, O Exalter,
exalt my dhikr by making me follow guidance.

مُعِزُّ مُذِلٌّ يَا سَمِيعُ بَصِيرُ جُدْ

عَلَىٰ مَا تَرَىٰ مِنْ فَادِح الْعَيْبِ بِالسِّتْرِ

O Enacter, O One Who humbles, O Hearing O Seeing,
Draw Your veil and cover the ugliness of my faults.

وَيَا حَكَمُ عَدْلُ لَطِيفُ خَبِيرُ مَا

لَنَا وَزَرُ إِلَّاكَ فِي الضَّيِّقِ وَالْعُسْرِ

O the Just, O the Judge, the Latif, Aware of all things,
We are overcome unless we have You in distress and hardship.

حَلِيمٌ عَظِيمٌ يَا غَفُورُ شَكُورُ لَنْ

يَخِيبَ امْرُؤًا يَرْجُوكَ بِالحِلْمِ وَالْغَفْرِ

O Indulgent, Immense, Utterly Forgiving, Grateful,
You do not disappoint the one who hopes for gentle pardon from You.

عَلِيٌّ كَبِيرُ يَا حَفِيظُ مُقِيتُ هَبْ

لَنَا حِفْظَكَ الأَحْمَى لَدَى الْحَادِثِ الْوَعْرِ

O High, Great, All-Preserver, Nourisher, grant us
Your sheltering protection in every difficult event.

حَسِيبُ جَلِيلُ يَا رَقِيبُ كَرِيمُ مَنْ

سِوَاكَ نُرَجِّيهِ لِحَلَّةِ ذِي فَقْرِ

O All-Reckoning, Majestic, Ever-Watchful, Generous,
who other than You can we hope will be a friend for one in poverty?

مُجِيبُ أَجِبْ يَا وَاسِعُ يَا حَكِيمُ يَا

وَدُودُ دُعَا دَاعٍ لِفَضْلِكَ مُضْطَرِّ

O Answerer, Utterly Vast beyond measure, Ever-Wise, Loving,
answer the prayers of the one who, hard-pressed, prays for Your bounty.

مَجِيدُ بِجُدْ يَا بَاعِثُ يَا شَهِيدُ بِا

لَّذِي نَرْتَجِي يَا حَقُّ مِنْ جُودِكَ الْغَمْرِ

O Glorious, Raiser of the Dead, Directly-perceiving Haqiqa,
by Whom we hope, be generous with Your all-engulfing generosity.

وَكِيلُ قَوِيٌّ يَا مَتِينُ وَلِيٌّ كُنْ

وَلِيًّا لِعَبْدٍ مِنْ خَطَايَاهُ فِي أَسْرِ

O Reliable Guardian, Overpoweringly Strong, Firm, Protector,
protect Your slave from falling into the captivity of wrong action.

حَمِيدُ وَمُحْصِي مُبْدِئٌ وَمُعِيدُ لَنْ

يَزَلْ مِنْكَ جُودٌ يَنْتَحِنَّ بِلَا حَصْرِ

O Praiseworthy, Knower of each separate thing, O Bringer-into-Being
and Bringer-Back, Your incalculable giving never ceases.

وَمُحْيِي مُمِيتٌ حَيٌّ قَيُّومٌ وَاجِدُ

وَيَا مَاجِدُ لَا تُوَلِّنِي الْخِزْيَ فِي النَّشْرِ

O Life-Giver, Life-Taker, Living, Self-Sustaining, Un-needing, All-Glorious,
do not assign me to punishment on the Day of Gathering.

وَيَا أَحَدُ نَرْجُوكَ يَا صَمَدُ إِذَا

تَضِيقُ بِنَا يَا قَادِرُ فُسْحَةُ الْعُمْرِ

O One, Self-Sufficient, All-Powerful Lord,
we have hope in You when the fullness of life becomes narrow.

وَمُقْتَدِرُ ارْفَعْ يَا مُقَدِّمُ رُتْبَتِي

مُؤَخِّرُ أَخِّرْ كُلَّ مَنْ يَبْتَغِي ضُرِّي

O Determiner, the Bringer-Near, the One Who puts it far, raise my rank
and put all who wish me harm far away from me.

وَيَا أَوَّلُ يَا آخِرُ ظَاهِرُ وَبَا

طِنُ وَالٍ اِجْذِبْنِي إِلَىٰ حَضْرَةِ الطُّهْرِ

O First, Last, Outwardly Manifest, Inwardly Hidden,
Protecting Master, draw me into the presence of purity.

وَيَا مُتَعَالِ بَرُّ تَوَّابُ جُدْ وَتُبْ

وَمُنْتَقِمُ حُلْ بَيْنَنَا وَذَوِي الشَّرِّ

O Sublime, Benign, Relenting – be generous to us and turn to us,
and, O Avenger, defend me against those who are evil.

عَفُوٌّ رَءُوفُ مَالِكُ الْمُلْكِ أَنْتَ ذُو

الْجَلَالِ وَالاِكْرَامِ اعْفُ عَنْ كُلِّ مَا وِزْرِ

O Effacer of wrong actions, All-Pitying, Possessor of the kingdom,
You are the Lord of Majesty and Gifts – forgive every wrong action.

وَمُقْسِطُ جَامِعُ غَنِيُّ فَأَغْنِنَا

غِنَى الْقَلْبِ يَا مُغْنِي لِنَغْنَ عَنِ الْوَفْرِ

O Equitable, O Gatherer, O Rich, Enricher,
enrich our hearts so that they may be rich to overflowing.

وَيَا مَانِعُ يَا ضَارُّ يا نَافِعُ اِهْدِنَا

بِنُورِكَ يَا نُورُ وَهَادٍ إِلَى الْيُسْرِ

O Preventer, Harmer, and Benefitter, Light and Guide –
guide us by Your light to tranquillity.

بَدِيعُ وَبَاقٍ وَارِثُ يَا رَشِيدُ يَا
صَبُورُ أَتِحْ لِي الرُّشْدَ لِلشُّكْرِ وَالصَّبْرِ

O Originator, O Enduring, Inheritor, Infallible-Guide,
All-Patient, give me right guidance in gratitude and fortitude.

بِأَسْمَائِكَ الْحُسْنَىٰ دَعَوْنَاكَ نَبْتَغِي
رِضَاكَ وَلُطْفًا فِي الْحَيَاةِ وَفِي الْقَبْرِ

We beg You by Your most beautiful Names,
seeking Your approval and lutf in this life and the grave.

وَفِي النَّشْرِ ثُمَّ الْحَشْرِ وَالْمَوْقِفِ الَّذِي
تُحَاسِبُ فِيهِ الْخَلْقَ يَا عَالِمَ السِّرِّ

And on the Day of Rising and Gathering at the stopping place
where creation will be taken to account, O Knower of secrets!

وَفِي حَالِ أَخْذِ الصُّحْفِ وَالْوَزْنِ بَعْدَهَا
كَذَالِكَ فِي حَالِ الْمُرُورِ عَلَى الْجَسْرِ

When the books of actions are taken and weighed
and at the arrival and when we pass over the bridge.

وَعَافِيَةَ دِينًا وَدُنْيَا وَرَحْمَةً
بِفَضْلِكَ فِي الدَّارَيْنِ يَا وَاسِعَ الْبِرِّ

O Vast in Goodness, give us health in our Deen,
and this world, and mercy in the two abodes by Your generosity.

وَخَتْماً بِحُسْنَىٰ مَعْ جِوَارِ نَبِيِّنَا

مُحَمَّدٍ الْمَحْمُودِ فِي الْمَوْقِفِ الْحَشْرِ

We ask for a seal of goodness, and to be near the Prophet Muhammad,
the Praiseworthy, in the Station of Gathering.

عَلَيْهِ صَلَاةُ اللهِ ثُمَّ سَلَامُهُ

بِلَا مُنْتَهَىٰ وَالْآلِ مَعْ صَحْبِهِ الْغُرِّ

May the blessings of Allah be upon him, and His peace without end,
and on his family and glorious Companions.

وَلِلنَّاظِمِ اغْفِرْ يَا إِلَهِي وَأَهْلِهِ

وَأَحْبَابِهِ وَاسْتُرْهُمْ دَائِمَ السِّتْرِ

O my God, pardon the poet and his family and loved ones,
and always veil and conceal their wrong actions,

وَقَارِئِهَا وَالْمُسْلِمِينَ جَمِيعِهِمْ

وَلِلَّهِ رَبِّ دَائِمُ الْحَمْدِ وَالشُّكْرِ ۞

And pardon the reader and all the Muslims.
Praise and thanks endlessly belongs to Allah, my Lord.

The Salat of Ibn Mashish
الصلاة المشيشية

اَللّٰهُمَّ صَلِّ عَلَى مَنْ مِنْهُ انْشَقَّتِ الاَسْرَارُ. وَانْفَلَقَتِ الاَنْوَارُ.
وَفِيهِ ارْتَقَتِ الْحَقَائِقُ. وَتَنَزَّلَتْ عُلُومُ سَيِّدِنَا ءَادَمَ عَلَيْهِ السَّلَامُ
فَأَعْجَزَ الْخَلَائِقَ. وَلَهُ تَضَاءَلَتِ الْفُهُومُ
فَلَمْ يُدْرِكْهُ مِنَّا سَابِقٌ وَلَا لَاحِقٌ

O Lord, bless him, out of whom secrets and lights have burst, in whom
rose the truth, upon whom devolved the knowledge of our master
Adam, peace be upon him. Beside him all creatures are incapable, to
him understanding is a trifle. Not one of us has attained his standard,
before or after.

فَرِيَاضُ الْمَلَكُوتِ بِزَهْرِ جَمَالِهِ مُونِقَةٌ.
وَحِيَاضُ الْجَبَرُوتِ بِفَيْضِ أَنْوَارِهِ مُتَدَفِّقَةٌ.

The gardens of heaven are embellished with the beauty of his flowers.
The cisterns of power spill over with the flood of his lights.

وَلَا شَيْءَ إِلَّا وَهُوَ بِهِ مَنُوطٌ. إِذْ لَوْ لَا الْوَاسِطَةُ لَذَهَبَ كَمَا قِيلَ
الْمَوْسُوطُ. صَلَاةً تَلِيقُ بِكَ مِنْكَ إِلَيْهِ كَمَا هُوَ أَهْلُهُ.

There is nothing not dependent on him: for as it was said, 'without the
means the end would have escaped us'.
Bless him in Your way according to his merits.

اَللّٰهُمَّ إِنَّهُ سِرُّكَ الْجَامِعُ الدَّالُّ عَلَيْكَ.

وَحِجَابُكَ الْاَعْظَمُ الْقَآئِمُ لَكَ بَيْنَ يَدَيْكَ.

O Allah, he is your gathered secret that tells of You,
Your great veil that stands before You.

اَللّٰهُمَّ أَلْحِقْنِي بِنَسَبِهِ. وَحَقِّقْنِي بِحَسَبِهِ. وَعَرِّفْنِي إِيَّاهُ مَعْرِفَةً أَسْلَمُ

بِهَا مِنْ مَوَارِدِ الْجَهْلِ. وَأَكْرَعُ بِهَا مِنْ مَوَارِدِ الْفَضْلِ.

O Allah, attach me to his descendants, and make me realise his honour. Let
me know him with a knowledge by means of which I will be safe from the
fountains of ignorance and bring me to the fountains of goodness.

وَاحْمِلْنِي عَلَى سَبِيلِهِ إِلَى حَضْرَتِكَ. حَمْلًا مَحْفُوفًا بِنَصْرَتِكَ. وَاقْذِفْ

بِي عَلَى الْبَاطِلِ فَأَدْمَغَهُ. وَزُجَّ بِي فِي بِحَارِ الْاَحَدِيَّةِ. وَانْشُلْنِي مِنْ

أَوْحَالِ التَّوْحِيدِ. وَأَغْرِقْنِي فِي عَيْنِ بَحْرِ الْوَحْدَةِ. حَتَّى لَاۤ أَرَى

وَلَاۤ أَسْمَعَ وَلَاۤ أَجِدَ وَلَاۤ أُحِسَّ إِلَّا بِهَا.

Convey me on his way to Your Presence, protected by Your help. Let me
face falsehood so that I may conquer it, drive me into the sea of Oneness,
snatch me from the mires of belief in Unification (Tawhid) and let me
drown in the sea of Unity (Wahda) so much that I may not see, hear,
feel or sense except by It.

وَاجْعَلِ الْحِجَابَ الْاعْظَمَ حَيَاةَ رُوحِي. وَرُوحَهُ سِرَّ حَقِيقَتِي.
وَحَقِيقَتَهُ جَامِعَ عَوَالِمِي بِتَحْقِيقِ الْحَقِّ الاوَّلِ.

Make the great veil the life of my spirit and its spirit the secret of my truth
and his truth, the integrator of my universe through the realisation of the
first truth.

يَآ أَوَّلُ يَآ ءَاخِرُ يَا ظَاهِرُ يَا بَاطِنُ.

O First! O Last! O Manifest! O Hidden!

اِسْمَعْ نِدَآئِي بِمَا سَمِعْتَ بِهِ نِدَاءَ عَبْدِكَ سَيِّدِنَا زَكَرِيَّاءَ عَلَيْهِ السَّلَامُ.
وَانْصُرْنِي بِكَ لَكَ. وَأَيِّدْنِي بِكَ لَكَ. وَاجْمَعْ بَيْنِي وَبَيْنَكَ.
وَحُلْ بَيْنِي وَبَيْنَ غَيْرِكَ.

Hear my cry as you heard the cry of Your slave, our master Zakariah,
peace be upon him. Give me victory through You – for You. Support
me through You – for You. Join me to You – separate me from other-
than-You.

اللهُ اللهُ اللهُ

ALLAH (3)

إِنَّ الَّذِي فَرَضَ عَلَيْكَ الْقُرْءَانَ لَرَآدُّكَ إِلَىٰ مَعَادٍ.

He Who has imposed the Qur'an upon you will surely bring you home
again.

رَبَّنَا ءَاتِنَا مِنْ لَدُنْكَ رَحْمَةً وَهَيِّئْ لَنَا مِنْ أَمْرِنَا رَشَدًا. (ثلاثًا)

Our Lord, give us mercy directly from You and open the way for us to
right guidance in our situation. (3)

From the Diwan
of Shaykh Muhammad al-Fayturi Hamuda

مِن ديوان الشيخ محمد الفيتوري حمودة

1

Ya taliba-l-ma'rifa

يَا طَالِبَ الْمَعْرِفَه   وَمَقَامَاتِ الصَّفَا
اِصْحَبْ خِلًّا قَدْ وَفَىٰ   بِعُبُودِيَّةِ اللّٰه

O seeker of gnosis and the stations of serenity!
Keep the company of a close friend
who has fully met the obligation of slavehood to Allah.

لَا تَكْتَفِ بِالْاَقْوَالْ   اِنْهَضْ بَادِرْ بِالْاَعْمَالْ
تَبْلُغْ مَقَامَ الْكَمَالْ   لَا إِلَهَ إِلَّا اللّٰه

Do not be content with words. Arise and embark on deeds without delay!
You will reach the Station of perfection – there is no god except Allah.

وَإِنْ تُرِيدُ الْمَعْنَىٰ   فِي اسْمِ ذَاتِهِ فَافْنَىٰ
كَرِّرًا مُعْلِنًا   تُحْظَىٰ بِلِقَاءِ اللّٰه

If you desire the meaning, then seek annihilation in the name of His essence.
Often and openly – you will obtain encounter with Allah.

بِهِ تَبْلُغُ الْمَقْصُودْ ۝ تُسْقَى بِكَأْسِ الشُّهُودْ

فَتَرَى كُلَّ الْوُجُودْ ۝ ظَاهِراً بِنُورِ اللهِ

You will obtain the goal by it –

you will be given the cup of witnessing to drink.

Then you will see all of existence outwardly manifest by the light of Allah.

اذْكُرْهُ مَعْنًى وَحِسّْ ۝ مِنْ النُّورِ تَقْتَبِسْ

تَدْخُلْ فِي مَقَامِ الانْسْ ۝ دَائِماً فَرْحَكْ بِاللهِ

Remember Him in meaning and the senses – you will acquire light.

You will enter the Station of intimacy – your joy constantly with Allah.

قُلِ اللهُ جَهْرَةً ۝ وَسِرّاً وَخَلْوَةً

فَيَأْتِيكَ نَفْحَةٌ ۝ تُفْنِيكَ فِي ذَاتِ اللهِ

Say 'Allah!' openly, secretly, and in retreat,

A breath of fragrance will come to you

which will annihilate you in the essence of Allah.

رَاقِبْ جَمَالَ الْحَبِيبْ ۝ هُوَ الْقَرِيبُ الْمُجِيبْ

يَأْتِيكَ فَتْحٌ غَرِيبْ ۝ تُحْيَ بِشُهُودِ اللهِ

Watch the beauty of the Beloved with fear –

He is the Near, the Answerer –

A startling opening will come to you –

you will be brought to life by the witnessing of Allah.

تَوَضَّأْ بِمَاءِ الْغَيْبْ　وَيَمِّمْ نَحْوَ الْحَبِيبْ

فَثَمَّ سِرٌّ عَجِيبْ　تَشْهَدِ اللهَ بِاللهْ

Do wudu with the water of the unseen
and direct yourself toward the Beloved.
There is a wondrous secret! You will see Allah by Allah!

وَإِنْ تُرِيدِ التَّمْكِينْ　وَأَذْوَاقَ الْعَارِفِينْ

أُسْتَاذِي عَيْنُ التَّعِيينْ　الْعَلَوِي سِرُّ اللهْ

If you desire the firm establishment and the tasting of the gnostics,
My master is the very one designated, al-'Alawi, the secret of Allah.

فَهَيَّمَنِي بِالْوِدَادْ　مِنْهُ أَتَتْنِي الْإِمْدَادْ

فَنِلْتُ أَعْلَا الْمُرَادْ　صِرْتُ غَنِيًّا بِاللهْ

He bewildered me in love. Help has come to me from him,
So I obtained the highest desire – I became rich in Allah.

يَا مَنْ تُرِيدِ الدَّوَا　وَالْغَيْبَ عَنِ السِّوَىٰ

اِشْرَبْ مِنْ خَمْرِي تُرْوَىٰ　فَتَنْظُرْ جَمَالَ اللهْ

O you who desire the cure and withdrawal from other!
Drink from my wine and you will be quenched.
Then you will see the beauty of Allah.

تَبْرُزْ لَكَ شُمُوسُ الذَّاتْ بِالاَسْمَاءِ وَالصِّفَاتْ

فِي جَمِيعِ الْكَائِنَاتْ كَانَ اللّٰهْ وَبَاقِ اللّٰهْ

The suns of the essence will bring you the names and the attributes
in all beings. Allah was and Allah remains.

حَدِّدْ بَصَرَ الاِيمَانْ تَرَى اللّٰهَ لَا الاَكْوَانْ

هٰذَا مَقَامُ الاِحْسَانْ اِخْتِصَاصًا مِنَ اللّٰهْ

Make the eye of Iman keen –
you will see Allah, not phenomenal beings.
This is the Station of Ihsan, a special favour from Allah.

لَا بِجِدٍّ وَاجْتِهَادْ عَطَاءٌ مِنَ الْجَوَادْ

اَلرَّؤُوفُ بِالْعِبَادْ شُكْرًا وَحَمْدًا لِلّٰهْ

Not by diligence or striving – a gift from the Generous,
the Compassionate to the slaves. Thanks and praise be to Allah!

مُحَمد الْفَيتُورِي مُعتَرِفْ بِالْقُصُورِ

بِهِ تَمَّ سُرُورِي فَانٍ وَبَاقِ بِالله

Muhammad al-Fayturi admits his incapacity,
In Him my happiness was complete – annihilated and going-on in Allah.

220

صَلِّ مَوْلَانَا الْعَظِيمْ   عَلَى الرَّؤُوفِ الرَّحِيمْ

هُوَ الصِّرَاطُ الْقَوِيمْ   هَادِيًا بِإِذْنِ اللهْ ﴿۝﴾

Our Master, the Great, bless the gentle, the merciful.
He is the straight path, guiding by the permission of Allah.

2

Adramat naru-l-hawa

أَضْرَمَتْ نَارُ الْهَوَىٰ   لَدَعَتْ قَلْبِي انْكَوَىٰ

لَنْ تَذَرْ فِيهِ السِّوَىٰ   عَادَ فَرْعِي لِأَصْلِي

The fire of passion was kindled and it called my heart: Be burned!
It will not leave other in it, so it became a branch of my root.

خِلِّي ظَاهِرٌ فِي مَجْلَاهْ   أَضَاءَ الْكَوْنَ سَنَاهْ

ظَهَرَتْ شَمْسُ بَهَاهْ   مَا أَبْدَعُ التَّجَلِّي

My close Friend is outwardly manifest in His place of tajalli.
The cosmos illuminated His radiance.
The sun of His splendour appeared – how marvellous the tajalli is!

فَهُوَ سِرُّ الْوُجُودْ   هُوَ الشَّاهِدْ وَالْمَشْهُودْ

إِلَـيْهِ الأَمْرُ يَعُـودْ   هُوَ مُرْشِدُ الْكُلِّ

He is the secret of existence. He is the Witness and the Witnessed.
The command returns to Him. He is the guide of all.

أَوْقَاتِي بِهِ هَنَا   لَمَّا فَهِمْتُ الْمَعْنَى

حَبِيبِي مِنِّي دَنَا   وَمَطْلُوبِي حَصَلْ لِي

My moments were full of delight with Him
when I understood the meaning –
My Beloved drew near me and my goal was obtained for me.

أَطْلَقَنِي مِنَ الْقُيُودْ   سَقَانِي كَأْسَ الشُّهُودْ

سِوَاهُ عِنْدِي مَفْقُودْ   مِنْهُ نُطْقِي وَفِعْلِي

He freed me of fetters and let me drink from the glass of witnessing.
Other-than-Him is lost with me. My speech and action is from Him.

شَرِبْتُ خَمْرَ الاذْوَاقْ   مِنْ رَاحَتْ سَاقِي الْعُشَّاقْ

بَرَزَتْ شَمْسُ الاطْلَاقْ   بَدَى حُسْنُ التَّحَلِّي

I drank the wine of tasting
from the hands of the cupbearer of the passionate ones.
The sun of liberation emerged and the beauty of adornment appeared.

نَظَرْتُ خَلْفَ السِّتَارْ   مَا لَا تُدْرِكُ الابْصَارْ

غِبْتُ فِي بَحْرِ الانْوَارْ   صَارَ بَعْضِي كُلِّي

I looked behind the veil at what the eyes do not perceive,
I withdrew into the sea of lights – part of me became all of me.

دَارَتْ كُؤُوسُ الطَّرِيقْ   أُدْنُ مِنِّي يَا رَفِيقْ

نُسْقِيكَ خَمْرَ عَتِيقْ   تُحْظَىٰ بِرُوجِ الْكُلِّ

The goblets of the Path were passed around:
'Come near Me, My friend!
We will let you drink an ancient wine – you will obtain the joy of all!'

أُسْتَاذِي نُقْطَةُ الْبَاءْ   مِنْهُ كَانَ الِابْتِدَاءْ

ظُهُورًا وَانْتِهَا   فَافْهَمُو يَا عُذَّالِي

My master is the dot of the ba'. The beginning was from him,
Outwardly as well as at the end. Understand then, O critic!

هَلُّوا أَهْلَ الْعِرْفَانْ   إِلَىٰ مِنْهَلِ الْإِحْسَانِ

اَلْعَلَوِي غَوْثُ الزَّمَانْ   بِهِ تَمَّ وِصَالِي

People of gnosis! Come now to the spring of Ihsan!
Al-'Alawi, the ghawth of the age. My arrival was completed by him.

فَهُوَ فَخْرُ الاَسْرَارْ   وَهُوَ الْكَأْسُ وَانْخَمَارْ

وَهُوَ السَّاقِي لِلاَحْبَارِ   مِنْ خَمْرَةِ الْكَمَالِ

He is the glory of the secrets. He is the glass and the wine.
He is the Cupbearer of the wine of perfection to the learned.

فَيتَورِي بِهِ وَلْهَانْ   شَارِبْ مِنْ خَمْرِهْ نَشْوَانْ

إِنِّي لَفَرْدُ الزَّمَانْ   عَبْدًا بِلَا انْفِصَالِ

Al-Fayturi is out of his head with love from him —

he drinks intoxicated from his wine.

I am an individual of the age, a slave without interruption.

فَصَلُّوا يَا فُقَرَا   عَلَى أَعْظَمِ الْوَرَى

خَيرُ مَنْ بِهِ أَسْرِي   مَغْنَاطِيسُ الْكَمَّالِ ﴿۞﴾

Fuqara! Then ask for blessings on the greatest of mankind,

The best, by whom the magnet of perfection flows!

3

Tajalla Hibbi

تَجَلَّى حِبِّي   اِفْرَح يَا قَلْبِي

اِحْرِمْ وَلْبِي   بَجْرِي تبسم

My Beloved appeared to me in tajalli! Rejoice, my heart!
Divest yourself while my core, my glory smiles.

غَرَامِي زَاد   سَاقِيهِ نَادَىٰ

أَخْذَ الْفُؤَادَ   بِالْحَفْضِ وَالضَّم

My passion increased – His cupbearer called –
He took the heart with joining and subduing.

دَارَتْ كُؤُوسِي أَحْيَتْ نُفُوسِي

لَاحَتْ شُمُوسِي مِنْ حُلْوِ الْمَبْسَمْ

My cups went around – my selves gave life –
my suns shone because of the sweetness of the smile.

هُوَ حَيَاتِي مَحْوَىٰ ثَبَاتِي

أَفْنَ فِي الذَّاتِ لِلسَّيْرِ تَفْهَمْ

He is my life, the focus of my firmness —
annihilate yourself in the essence for the journey,
then you will understand!

مَوْتِي وُجُودِي غَيْبِي شُهُودِي

فَالْجُودُ جُودِي وَالْحَيْرَه تَمْتَمْ

My death is my existence, my withdrawal is my witnessing —
so generosity is my generosity and confusion stutters.

هَذَا تَلْوِينِي فِي كُلِّ حِينٍ

أَبْصَرْ بِعَيْنِي لِكَنْزِكَ تَغْنَمْ

This is my sign in every time.
Look with my eye at your treasure, you will obtain booty.

أُنْظُرْ فِي ذَاتِكْ تَحْيَا حَيَاتَكْ

رُوحُكْ نَادَاتِكْ لِفَكَّ الطَّلْسَمْ

Look at your essence — you will be brought to life by your life.
Your spirit called to you to unwind the talisman.

سِرُّ الْهِدَايَه كَهْفُ الْوِلَايَه

سَيِّدِي مَوْلَايَ لِلْكُلِّ أَنعِم

The secret of guidance is the cavern of wilaya,
my master, my lord giving favours to all.

الْعُرْوَةُ الْوَثِيقَه عَيْنُ الطَّرِيقَه

كَنْزُ الْحَقِيقَه الْفَرْدُ الْخَاتَم

The firm grip, the source of the Path,
the treasury of the Haqiqa, the unique individual, the seal.

هُوَ سُلْطَانِي فِي كُلِّ آنٍ

شَمْسُ الْعِرْفَانِ الْعَلَوِي الاَعْظَم

He is my sultan at every moment,
the sun of gnosis, al-'Alawi, the greatest.

صَرِّحْ يَا حَادِي فِي كُلِّ نَادِ

عُبَيْدُ أَسْيَادِي الْفِيتُورِي فَاعْلَم

Announce, caravan leader! to every circle
the little slave of my lords, al-Fayturi, and learn!

صَلِّ يَا رَبّ عَلَى الْمُرَبِّي

أَحْيَا لِي قَلْبِي بِفَكِّ الطَّلْسَمْ ۝

O Lord! Bless the one who tends

he brought my heart to life by unwinding the talisman.

4

Nadani Hibbi

نَادَانِي حِبِّي مِنْ حَضْرَهْ قُرْبِي

قُمْتُ مُلَبِّي لِنِدَاءِ اللهْ

My Beloved called me from the presence of my nearness —
I stood up to answer the call of Allah.

أَتَيْتُ لِلْبَابْ مِنْ غَيْرِ ارْتِيَابْ

وَجَدْتُ الاَحْبَابْ فِي حَضْرَةِ اللهْ

I came to the door without hesitation
I found the lovers in the presence of Allah.

شَرِبْتُ بِالاَقْدَاحْ مِنْ دَنْدَاتِ الرَّاحْ

فَاهْتَزَّتِ الاَشْبَاحْ طَرَبًا بِاللهْ

I drank cups from the wine-jars of joy,
so the forms quivered out of rapture with Allah.

شَرَابٌ قَدِيمٌ ۚ قَدْرُهُ عَظِيمٌ

صِرَاطٌ قَوِيمٌ ۚ لِمُرِيدِ اللّٰهْ

A timeless drink whose value is immense,
a straight path for the one who desires Allah.

طَلَعَ الصَّبَاحْ ۚ بِنُورِ الْفَلَاحْ

صِرْنَا بِالْاَرْوَاحْ ۚ مِنْ مَلَكُوتِ اللّٰهْ

The morning came with the light of success –
we went with the spirits from the Malakut of Allah.

لَاقَيْنَا الْحَكِيمْ ۚ اَلْغَوْثَ الْعَظِيمْ

اَلْعَلَوِي الْمُقِيمْ ۚ فِي جَبَرُوتِ اللّٰهْ

We met the wise, the great ghawth,
al-'Alawi, residing in the Jabarut of Allah.

لِكَوْنِي طَوَىٰ ۚ فَغَابَ السِّوَىٰ

فَقُلْتُ هُوَ ۚ هُوَ هُوَ اللّٰهْ

He crossed to my being and Other withdrew.
Then I said: He! He! He! Allah!

231

نَاصِحُ الأُمَّةْ مُجَلِّي الغُمَّةْ

صَاحِبُ الهِمَّةْ فِي طَرِيقِ اللهْ

The counsellor of the community, he who manifests sorrow,
the possessor of himma in the Path of Allah.

وَارِثُ الرَّسُولْ بِالفِعْلِ وَالقَوْلْ

حَضْرَةُ القَبُولْ لأَحْكَامِ اللهْ

The heir of the Messenger in action and word,
the presence of acceptance of the judgments of Allah.

سَيْفُ الإِسْلَامِ مُحِي الأَنَامِ

حَازَ الْمَقَامِ اِصْطَفَاهُ اللهْ

The sword of Islam, the reviver of people,
he won the station which Allah chose.

آدَمُ الزَّمَانْ خَلَّفَهُ الرَّحْمَنْ

لَا تَكُنْ شَيْطَانْ تُشْقَى بِلِقَاهْ

The Adam of the age whom the Merciful made a Khalifa.
Do not be a shaytan, you will have trouble when you meet him.

أَتَوْا إِلَيْهِ   وَهِيمُوا بِهِ
خَرُّوا إِلَيْهِ   سُجَّدًا لِلَّهْ

They came to him and thirsted with passionate love for him.
They swooned before him, prostrating to Allah.

أَسْكَرْنِي شَذَاهْ   حَيَّرَنِي مَعْنَاهْ
أَدْهَشَنِي بَهَاهْ   سَجَدْتُ لِلَّهْ

His fragrance intoxicated me and his meaning put me in confusion –
his radiance dazzled me, I prostrated to Allah.

يَا مُرِيدْ أَقْدِمْ   إِنْ شِئْتَ تَغْنَمْ
اذْكُرْ وَسَلِّمْ   تَحْظَى بِلِقَاهْ

O murid! Advance if you desire booty!
Do dhikr and greet, you will obtain his encounter.

غِبْ عَنِ الصِّفَاتْ   وَأَفْنَ فِي الذَّاتْ
تُحْيِيكَ الْحَيَاهْ   تَبْقَى بِبَقَاهْ

Withdraw from the attributes and annihilate yourself in the essence
– it will bring you completely to life and you will go on
with His going-on.

صَلِّ يَا سَلَامْ   عَلَى قُطْبِ الاَنَامْ

بِهِ قَلْبِي هَامْ   فُزْتُ بِلِقَاهْ ۞

O peace! Bless the pole of men!

My heart thirsts after him with passionate love, so I won his encounter.

5

Utruk ya murid

أُتْرُكْ يَا مُرِيدْ   نَفْسَكَ مَا تُرِيدْ

إِنْ رُمْتَ الْمَزِيدْ   مِنْ أَسْرَارِ اللّٰهْ

O murid! Abandon your self and what it wants
if you desire increase from the secrets of Allah!

أُدْخُلِ الطَّرِيقْ   وَالْزَمِ الرَّفِيقْ

يُسْقِيكَ الْعَتِيقْ   مِنْ خَمْرَةِ اللّٰهْ

Enter the path and cling to the friend –
he will give you an ancient vintage of the wine of Allah to drink.

يُعْطِيكَ الْحَبِيبْ   سِرَّهُ الْعَجِيبْ

هِمْ بِهِ وَغِبْ   فِي أَنْوَارِ اللّٰهْ

The Beloved will give you His wondrous secret –
thirst with love for him and withdraw into the lights of Allah.

ذَابَتِ الاشْبَاحْ لَمَّا حِبِّي بَاحْ
بِاسْمِ الْفَتَّاحْ لِمُرِيدِ اللهْ

The forms melted away when my Beloved divulged
the name of opening for the one who desires Allah.

دَارَتِ الاقْدَاحْ بَيْنَنَا يَا صَاحْ
فَاحَ السِّرُّ فَاحْ مِنْ مِشْكَاةِ اللهْ

The cups went around among us, O friend,
the secret diffused a fragrant scent from the niche of Allah.

أَدْنَ لَدُنِ الرَّاحْ شُرْبِه مُبَاحْ
بِهِ حَقًّا تَرْتَاحْ تَرَىٰ وَجْهَ اللهْ

Draw near to the wine whose drink is permitted.
By it you will truly be pleased, you will see the face of Allah.

اِرْجِعْ يَا جَاحِدْ فَلَا تُعَانِدْ
لِلْفَرْدِ الْمُرْشِدْ هُوَ نُورُ اللهْ

O denier! Refrain and do not be stubborn
towards the unique individual, the guide who is the light of Allah.

يُرَبِّي بِالنَّظْرَه ۚ يُدَخِّلْ لِلْحَضْرَه

صَاحِبُ الاِسْرَا ۚ فِي جَبَرُوتِ اللّه

He teaches with the glance and he admits

the possessor of the night-journey in the Jabarut of Allah to the Presence.

فَهِمْتُ بِهِ ۚ مِنْهُ إِلَيْهِ

مَنْ ذَا يُدْرِيهِ ۚ جَامِعَ سِرِّ اللّه

I understood by him, from him, to him

whoever knows him to contain the secret of Allah.

مِنْهَجُ الطَّرِيقْ ۚ سُلْطَانُ التَّحْقِيقْ

فَنِعْمَ الرَّفِيقْ ۚ لِمُرِيدِ اللّه

The open road of the Path, the Sultan of realisation!

How excellent is the friend for the one who desires Allah!

اَلْعَلَوِي سَيِّدِي ۚ إِبْنُ الْبُوزِيدِي

أَطْلَقْ لِي قَيْدِي ۚ أَصْبَحْتُ لِلَّه

Al-'Alawi is my master, the son of al-Buzidi.

He set me free from my fetters and I was sent forth to the company of Allah.

عَرَّفْنِي نَفْسِي   أَدْخَلْنِي أُنْسِي

فِي حَضْرَه قُدْسِي   غِبْتُ عَنْ سِوَاه

He made me recognise my self, he made me enter my intimacy –
I withdrew from other-than-Him in the presence of purity.

فَيْتُورِي سَقِيمْ   أَتَىٰ بِالتَّسْلِيمْ

لِلْغَوْثِ الْعَظِيمْ   مِنْهَل عِلْمِ اللهْ

Fayturi is wasting-away and brings the greeting
to the great Ghawth, the spring of the knowledge of Allah.

صَلِّ الْمَوْلَىٰ   عَلَىٰ نُورِ الْهُدَىٰ

أَحْيَا لِي قَلْبِي   شَاهَدْتُ الْمَوْلَىٰ ۞

May the Master bless the light of guidance!
He brought my heart to life and I saw the Master.